A Practical Guide to World Philosophies

Bloomsbury Introductions to World Philosophies

Series Editor:

Monika Kirloskar-Steinbach

Assistant Series Editor:

Leah Kalmanson

Regional Editors

Nader El-Bizri, James Madaio, Sarah A. Mattice, Takeshi Morisato, Pascah Mungwini, Omar Rivera, and Georgina Stewart

Bloomsbury Introductions to World Philosophies delivers primers reflecting exciting new developments in the trajectory of world philosophies. Instead of privileging a single philosophical approach as the basis of comparison, the series provides a platform for diverse philosophical perspectives to accommodate the different dimensions of cross-cultural philosophizing. While introducing thinkers, texts, and themes emanating from different world philosophies, each book, in an imaginative and pathbreaking way, makes clear how it departs from a conventional treatment of the subject matter.

Forthcoming Titles in the Series:

A Practical Guide to World Philosophies, by Monika Kirloskar-Steinbach and Leah Kalmanson

Daya Krishna and Twentieth-Century Indian Philosophy, by Daniel Raveh

Māori Philosophy, by Georgina Tuari Stewart

Li Zehou and Twentieth-Century Chinese Philosophy, by Andrew Lambert

Philosophy of Science and the Kyoto School, by Dean Anthony Brink

Samkhya and Classical Indian Philosophy, by Marzenna Jakubczak

Tanabe Hajime and the Kyoto School, by Takeshi Morisato

The Philosophy of the Brahma-sutra, by Aleksandar Uskokov

A Practical Guide to World Philosophies

Selves, Worlds, and Ways of Knowing

Monika Kirloskar-Steinbach
and Leah Kalmanson

BLOOMSBURY
NEW DELHI • LONDON • OXFORD • NEW YORK • SYDNEY

BLOOMSBURY INDIA
Bloomsbury Publishing India Pvt. Ltd
Second Floor, LSC Building No. 4, DDA Complex, Pocket C–6&7,
Vasant Kunj, New Delhi 110070

BLOOMSBURY, BLOOMSBURY ACADEMIC INDIA and the Diana logo are
trademarks of Bloomsbury Publishing Plc

First published in India 2024
First published in Great Britain 2021
Reprinted in 2021, 2023

Cover design by Louise Dugdale
Cover image © Christopher Chiavetta, The Wilderness, 2010 (acrylic and oil on paper, 32" × 32")

This edition published with permission from Bloomsbury Publishing Plc,
50 Bedford Square, London, WC1B3DP, UK

A catalogue record for this book is available from the British Library.
Library of Congress Cataloging-in-Publication Data

ISBN: 978-93-61317-99-6

Series: Bloomsbury Introductions to World Philosophies

Typeset by Deanta Global Publishing Services, Chennai, India

Printed at Manipal Technologies Limited, Manipal

To find out more about our authors and books
visit www.bloomsbury.com and sign up for our newsletters

Contents

Acknowledgments

Monika Kirloskar-Steinbach and Leah Kalmanson would like to thank Colleen Coalter at Bloomsbury Publishing for her advocacy, from the start, for the critical and creative aims of our book series *Introductions to World Philosophies*. Leah would like to acknowledge the abiding support she continues to receive from those faculty members in the Department of Philosophy at the University of Hawaiʻi at Mānoa who served on her dissertation committee in 2010: Vrinda Dalmiya, Roger Ames, Steve Odin, and Graham Parkes have always encouraged and enabled the kind of critical self-reflection that makes her work on the book series possible. Looking back even further, she wants to express her debt to her father Neil Kalmanson, whose vast collection of Asian philosophical texts in her childhood home in Georgia undoubtedly put her on the course she follows to this day.

Monika appreciates the role of her philosophical mentors in shaping her interests in philosophy. Both Ratan Karani in India and Hubert Schleichert in Germany taught her to be cognizant of the larger sociopolitical dimension of academic philosophy; the latter emboldened Monika to work on a more adequate conceptual framework for studying world philosophies. Her mother, an early supporter of the perspective developed in this book, welcomed the prospect of her daughter finally embarking on a book project for a nonspecialist audience. Although Kunda Kirloskar passed away shortly before this book's publication, she followed the book's making closely.

Finally, we are thankful to our series' regional editors for their support in shaping this series and for their long and rich conversations about world philosophies.

1

Why World Philosophies?

As our subtitle indicates, this introduction to "world philosophies" is also a book about selves, worlds, and ways of knowing. As such, it accomplishes two interrelated tasks: (1) it not only brings a world-philosophical approach to bear on these fundamental issues; but (2) it also shows how our very understanding of the meaning of the terms "selves," "worlds," and "knowing" is transformed in the process.

Although we intend for this volume to stand on its own as an exercise in world-philosophical practice, we have also designed it to serve as a guidebook to the Bloomsbury series *Introductions to World Philosophies*. The series is an educational resource that provides in-depth introductory texts in world-philosophical traditions appropriate for classroom use as well as accessible to a general audience. Each volume in the series responds to the thematic framework indicated in our subtitle, such that together the contributions provide a diverse array of philosophical perspectives on fundamental questions related to selves, world, and ways of knowing.

Recent years have seen a rise in interest in cross-cultural and comparative philosophy, evidenced by the publication of several volumes aimed largely at educators and academic philosophers. Notable titles include Tim Connolly's *Doing Philosophy Comparatively* (2015) and Bryan Van Norden's *Taking Back Philosophy: A Multicultural Manifesto* (2017). More than just multicultural textbooks, these volumes aim to specify comparative and cross-cultural methodologies, to address the persisting eurocentrism of academic philosophy at the structural level, and to propose models for a more diverse discipline moving forward. This book, and the Bloomsbury series as a whole, provides concrete resources to support these worthy initiatives. Although our work largely complements other recent offerings such as those mentioned earlier, we also propose interventions in standard comparative methodologies that distinguish members of the Bloomsbury series from other introductory texts. We hope that this volume clarifies our editorial vision for the series.

Throughout the book, we include detailed discussions of how the world-philosophical approach has transformed our concrete academic practices, from the theoretical and methodological considerations that have informed our decisions as series editors, to the pedagogical strategies we have adopted in our classrooms. We begin next with a preliminary overview of the concerns that motivated not only this book but the development of the series as a whole.

Standard Comparisons and Global Concerns

In 1949, nearly fifty philosophers from six different countries came together in Hawai'i following the invitation of the American philosopher and sinologist Charles Moore (1901–1967). Over six weeks, they explored how philosophical resources could contribute toward making a more peaceful postwar world. This conference was the second of its kind. In 1939, Moore had already organized a smaller meeting just before the full outbreak of the Second World War in Europe. A decade later, the need for peace had become more urgent. Many conference participants in Hawai'i were determined to use sources from world-philosophical traditions to ground world peace. By setting the stage for a dialogue between "the East" and "the West," the aim was to develop a "world perspective in philosophy, if not a world philosophy," as the Indian philosopher-statesman S. Radhakrishnan put it (1951: 4). This meeting is commonly considered to be at least one founding moment of "comparative philosophy" as we know it today in Europe and North America (cf. Kirloskar-Steinbach et al. 2014).

Today, more than half of a century later, the field seems to be poised to further enhance such a world perspective on philosophy. However, many specialists are becoming increasingly aware that this perspective necessitates significant changes in the hitherto practice of comparative philosophy. Some of these changes are about nomenclature. Take for example terms like "East" and "West." In general, they seem to suggest a neat and clean binary, a cleavage between the traditions subsumed under either side. Traditions associated with the "East" are typically described as having a deep spirituality that subordinates reason and lacks a general scientific attitude. Those linked up with the "West" are taken to be exemplars of reason, science, and material culture. This dichotomy, however, does not withstand further scrutiny.

Even a cursory study of recent world history indicates that ideological reasons have been largely instrumental in driving this supposedly neat bifurcation. Regions associated with the East (e.g., China, India, and Japan) are not solely "spiritual," nor have central Europe and North America, regions typically associated with the West, been the sole repositories of human reason, science, and/or material culture. Relatedly, the "East" and the "West" have intersected at different points over the last several centuries. As Sean Meighoo shrewdly observes,

> there is no "West," at least not in the sense in which it has been conceived as an altogether unique and distinctly privileged event or course of events within world history. Of course, this is also to say that there is no "East" or any other tradition in which we may situate ourselves completely outside the West, as it were. (2016: 12)

Specialists aiming for changes in the field are, however, not satisfied, with revisions in labels alone. They aim for a more substantial methodological reorientation. They object to a narrow—and biased—

understanding of comparative philosophy in which eurocentric philosophy serves as the default position of philosophy per se. In such an academic exercise, studies of non-European and non-Euro-American traditions are typically driven by questions such as: How best can "we" make "their" thought comprehensible to "us"? How do "they" fare according to "our" standards? Unsurprisingly, such a narrow focus often leads to simplistic results. When the dominant philosophical tradition is deployed as the measure against which the profundity of philosophical activity is judged, non-eurocentric traditions tend to be interpreted as "inferior" and "pale" precursors of the same. On the basis of such facile comparisons, it is then relatively easy to conclude that these traditions lack "original" philosophical content.

In other words, since the standard of comparison is predetermined, one simply mines the other position, text, or tradition for analogies, which can in some manner relate to established signposts in the dominant philosophical tradition. Such a comparative mode of inquiry does not enable the philosopher to dig deeper into conceptual, epistemological, and historiographical issues which would be salient in reconstructing the other tradition in all its facets. The comparativist remains trapped within the confines of her own, narrow, philosophical horizon. Her questions generate answers to issues by which she is already seized and which are determined by her own cultural conditioning. This narrow mode of inquiry does not allow her to face the possibility that the text, position, or tradition at hand could require that she ask totally different philosophical questions (Rosemont 1988: 66). Given that non-European and non-Euro-American traditions are approached through the prism of familiarity, traditions from near and afar begin to resemble each other. At best, their study will deliver (missing) parts of a mosaic that consists of the inquirers' own intellectual familiarities.

Cognizant of such difficulties, specialists aiming for a substantial methodological reset have begun to distance themselves from the term "comparative philosophy." Vrinda Dalmiya's sharp observations, for example, succinctly capture the main fault-lines of the standard comparativist mode:

> The "we have it too" approach attempted to show that whatever was found in the system we were comparing ours to, could be found in our theories as well; while the "what you say has been said by us before" approach went further by claiming that all the niceties of the other system had already been anticipated by mine: Comparative study was clearly an ideological battlefield to establish hegemonic power over whatever system of thought was not "ours." (2016: 292)

Given the history of post-Second World War comparative philosophy, several younger scholars—some of whom will be writing volumes in our series *Bloomsbury Introductions to World Philosophies*—are keen to heed Dalmiya's call to "engage with the messy issues of unjust privilege" being played out in the discipline (2016: 279). They attempt to critically contemplate their own power-encoded spaces when they do philosophy. Amy Donahue's methodological ruminations are a good example of such scholarship. Donahue leans on the postcolonial scholar Gayatri Chakravorty Spivak to alert us to how non-subaltern academics from affluent countries, who claim to be the true representatives of specific subaltern subjectivities in the academy, exploit the material advantages this representation brings to their own selves and careers. She writes: "[W]e should be alert to tendencies to render non-Western philosophies and philosophers sensible, not through their particularities, but as generic facsimiles of Western philosophies that are assumed by default to re-present universal philosophy" (2016: 602).

Rather than considering the very act of comparison to be a distinctive feature of their philosophizing, scholars like Donahue focus on the moral attitude that informs their work. Especially when engaging with unfamiliar, or even alien, philosophical and intellectual traditions, they strive to apply a combination of intellectual humility, respect, sincerity, and receptive generosity in such a manner to enable an "*unlearning* the presumptive privilege of one's own moral-intellectual traditions" and "*learning* something of the internal composition of questions and answers through which the relevant traditions of others have been historically shaped" (Scott 2012: 3).

Such attempts at realigning important parameters of the field are gaining traction. The increased use of singular terms like "global philosophy," "world philosophy," or "cross-cultural philosophy," and so on can be read as indicators of the general dissatisfaction with standard approaches in the field. This new labeling, one seems to hope, will draw attention to an "unbounded approach to philosophy," to a principled openness to the existence of philosophies all over the world (Brooks 2013: 258). However, these well-meaning labeling endeavors are not wholly plausible. "Global philosophy" and "world philosophy" seem to suggest that philosophy has always operated with one easily identifiable conceptual framework across space and time, which we call—and have always called—philosophy. Such a claim would be counterfactual. Indeed, recent scholarship—some of which will be referenced in the pages of this volume—attests to the plurality of conceptual frameworks adopted at different times and places. Furthermore, one salient, reductionist implication of a one-size-fits-all view of philosophy should be flagged. Attempts that marry the unbounded nature of philosophy with the notion of one conceptual framework may unwittingly reinscribe the very box such scholarship seeks to escape from (cf. Kalmanson 2015: 203). From different perspectives, thus, "any monological outlook is suspect in a genuinely *post*colonial and thus an open, messy, boundary-crossing world" (Kim 2019: 44).

For its part, the term "cross-cultural philosophy" seems to circumvent difficulties arising from the adoption of a singular conceptual framework, at least to some extent. It gestures toward a possible plurality of cultures in which philosophy is embedded. And yet, the term "culture" also carries its own colonial baggage. Driven by a representational view of knowing, cultures were isolated as supposedly separate, homogenous wholes. In many contexts, this representation was intertwined with complex colonial projects. Today, it is difficult to argue that culture is a neutral description for a particular way of life of a specific community. The "colonial processes of oppressive subjectification" continue to cast their shadow even over our supposedly neutral and impartial use of the term "culture" (Lugones 2010: 749).

World Philosophies and Global Concerns

Apparently, a term is needed which can easily and unambiguously indicate the presence of several "system[s] of ideas," which arose through reflection about our being in the world (Smart 1999: 7). The term "world philosophies" is an appropriate contender for the task at hand for several reasons.

1. The switch to the plural—"world philosophies" rather than "world philosophy"—signals an emphasis on the diversity of philosophical methodologies, intellectual lineages, and social contexts. Rather than following the conventional tack of being part of a single coherent discipline, the plural term allows for a variety of traditions that may overlap but not necessarily cohere. Indeed, even the possibility of radical incommensurability across traditions may be thus preserved.
2. It adequately captures the embodied nature of philosophizing. Philosophy is carried out by concrete bodies placed in specific, spatiotemporal, and socio-material contexts. In philosophizing, people make a concerted attempt at understanding the world around them from their own vantage-point in space and time. For this purpose, they make use of a conceptual vocabulary which has grown out of the humus of common customs and life-forms. Philosophical concepts have their own provenance

(cf. Janz 1996). They are generated in specific places for specific purposes. Philosophical activity, thus, cannot to be meaningfully separated from the historical and corporeal particularity of its epistemic subjects. A scholarship that is sensitive to the concrete conditions of existence and the life-practices of the horizon out of which philosophical discourse originates will engage with those particularized conditions.

3. The term "world philosophies" underscores that philosophizing is an "ever-present human possibility" (Salkever and Nylan 1994: 240). Arguably, human beings will converse about themselves and their place in the world as long as they continue to be present in it. So, a viable understanding of philosophy would not conceive it as an activity which is unique to a particular group at a particular point in time. The term "world philosophies" captures the ubiquity of philosophical activity as it relates to our being in the world—at different times and in different places. "Not all philosophizing takes the form of developing *a* philosophy in the sense of a relatively systematic worldview, any more than all dancing takes the form of performing *a* dance (a tango, say)" (Cooper 2018: 106).
4. The world-philosophies approach can rise to the challenges of what has in this context been called "philosophical neocolonialism" (Wiredu 1998: 153). Despite formal decolonization, curricula in the former colonies tend to be solely based on the eurocentric philosophical tradition. Philosophy students, whether in Accra, Auckland, Atlanta, Berlin, Laos, Mumbai, Nairobi, or Pretoria, continue to be nurtured on the same staple diet of thinkers like Immanuel Kant, Georg Wilhelm Friedrich Hegel, and Martin Heidegger. The salience of local philosophies to the life-worlds of these students is deemed to be largely irrelevant.

Even if one were to concede that the world-philosophies approach can indeed be helpful in placing plurality front and center, does it affect research output at all? Or does it merely signal a deliberate effort at refraining to use standard templates found in academic philosophy? Let us turn to these broader issues now.

A philosopher adopting a world-philosophies approach would be attentive to the possibility that the conceptual frameworks we tend to deploy in academic philosophy may be highly specific to the eurocentric context. After all, extant frameworks in the discipline have largely arisen within this specific context. Their claims to universality and objectivity notwithstanding, the scope of these frameworks is limited: "[P]hilosophical discourse itself originates from and is organically linked to the concrete conditions-of-existence and the life-practices of the horizon within and out of which it is formulated" (Serequeberhan 1994: 17).

When these frameworks are applied outside their own context, they may—due to their limited scope—face problems of applicability. An instructive example is Indigenous philosophies. In Māori philosophy, for example, all things have a life aspect; they are moments of creation. This so-called *mauri* dimension has been largely overshadowed in conventional takes on the Māori worldview for a particular reason: most of these have been preoccupied with juxtaposing this worldview with modern science. And, in line with standard tropes about "the West" and "the rest," any non-European and non-Euro-American paradigm is usually judged to be deficient when and where it deviates from the scientific presuppositions of so-called modernity. But as Georgina Stewart rightly points out, scholars operating with this cultural binary on both sides have not reflected that "both are cultural ways of knowing about the world." Instead, they have bought into the "grand epistemological claim" undergirding the singularity of science (2010: 73, 74). An "Indigenous science," as such, could only be seen as a totally incommensurable alternative to the modern eurocentric scientific paradigm.

Following Stewart's lead, a world-philosophies approach to Māori philosophy would on one hand exercise self-restraint in the use of extant philosophical categories, like science and nonscience. On the other hand, it would seek to home in on the specificity of Māori philosophy. Such a focus would reveal that a central value in Māori culture and knowledge is kinship between all living and nonliving natural things including humans, captured in the key concept of *whakapapa* ("genealogy"). *Whakapapa* sees all elements of nature as human kin, ancestors, or ancestor-gods, all the way up to the cosmic realm of Mother Earth, Papatūānuku, and Father Sky, Ranginui. *Whakapapa* is a central concept in the theoretical framework of Māori knowledge, and gives rise to values of respect and care for kin (cf. Stewart 2010: 79–80). One need not naively disregard the dominant scientific paradigm in order to see, at the least, that the Māori model asks us to reconsider our relation to this paradigm and our understanding of the world that such a paradigm purports to describe. In other words, by resisting the binary that puts "the West" alone on the side of science and progress, or that sets up a simplistic opposition between "pro-science" and "anti-science" worldviews, we can learn from Indigenous philosophies to gain a more complicated and nuanced perspective on contemporary issues of shared concern.

Historical reasons push one to deliberately exercise self-restraint or mindfulness in such inquiry. That the plurality of philosophical frameworks is largely absent from philosophy departments today may have more to do with sociopolitical factors related to capitalism and the use of modern technology than to the philosophical worth of those frameworks. Piggybacking on these sociopolitical factors, most (but not all) European philosophers simply denied the existence of any other sophisticated philosophy besides their own. Through this self-positioning, world philosophies were placed outside the fold of academic philosophy.

To deploy Charles Mills's well-known framing, this self-positioning led up to a "white ignorance," such that "false knowing" and "non-knowing" about people deemed "non-white" arose (2007: 20). The "Euro and later Euro-American reference group" was centered as "the constitutive norm" (2007: 25). Although other empires in human history have not shied away from using their hegemonic status to promote their own intellectual agendas, European philosophy's exclusivist policies are remarkable for a particular reason. Till today, its fallout continues to determine how academic departments are set up, not only in Europe and North America and but also in larger parts of the world.

It is precisely for this reason that some philosophers, especially those with ties to formerly colonized countries, are concerned about the "comprehensive epistemicide" that remains unabated (Lebakeng et al., 2006: 72). Given that the "dominant curriculum continues to be a source of alienation" (2006: 73), a palpable disconnect between academic frameworks and lived experiences arises. Epistemic resources which have been in place since colonial times cannot—and do not—make adequate sense of the experiences members of these societies have today (cf. Mungwini 2017). As a result of this hiatus, societal members lack the conceptual repertoire they would need to make sense of their own experiences. One reason for this malaise is that "due to political and economic factors, [. . .] the intellectuals of the observed cultures have themselves internalized the Western categories and standards of intelligibility so that they observe, understand and compare their own cultures in terms given to them by the West" (Daya Krishna 1986: 64).

A sustained study of world philosophies could help fix this problem. Attending to the actual place, the spatiotemporal context, in which a particular philosophy arose and thrived, could be useful in debunking the "myth of emptiness" (Mungwini 2017: 8). This multilayered myth operated under colonialism on several levels: it was used to claim foreign, supposedly vacant, and unowned land, and also to underscore the supposed singularity of European reason. By using local experiences (as also languages) to embark upon developing "veritable theories of knowledge" in the global context, one could then begin to subvert the "continued internalization of intellectual dependency" (2017: 13, 16). A sustained study of world philosophies could contribute to "epistemic liberation" in the former colonies inasmuch as it makes room for the development of conceptual frameworks which are better attuned to make sense of the experiences people are having in those particular contexts.

Notably, attempts at reconceptualizing professional philosophy are not restricted to former colonies. Within the eurocentric context itself, there are attempts directed toward changing a discipline that "has indeed become overly narrow, insulated from other disciplines, and in many quarters oblivious even to its own culture as well as to others" (Solomon and Higgins 2003: ix). For this reason, some philosophers challenge the "rules of control at work in the discursive practices of European Philosophy" (Outlaw 1996: 62). They demand that philosophers in general do a "better job of decolonizing ourselves from our mindsets as colonizers" (Bernasconi 1998: 293). This attempted decolonization goes further than the political act associated with the same name. It begins with a critical re-examination and rewriting of the history of professional philosophy to make place for currently marginalized traditions in academic philosophy (such as those emanating from Asian regions) as well as those that were previously said to be devoid of philosophical content (such as those indigenous to Africa, the Americas, Australia, and so on).

Now, some proponents of what is termed "epistemic decolonization" do not rest content with the track record of the field. They read this record as making slow, deliberately studied, attempts to assimilate content from non-Euro-American sources into the canon such that the latter's authority is not directly challenged. For these authors, such attempts are mere cosmetic changes, which are complicit in maintaining the status quo. As David Haekwon Kim underscores:

"Much that passes for epistemic decolonization, then, may only involve a *liberatory expansion of objects of inquiry* to accommodate concerns of the colonized, *not a centralizing of non-Western philosophies* in the theoretical framework itself. And by centralizing, I do not mean this in a purist way" (2019: 46–7; emphasis in the original).

Directing attention to the locality of philosophical knowledge-production processes, these scholars contend that philosophers have never been external, detached observers, but active participants involved in every step of the knowledge-producing process, be it in producing, certifying, or mediating knowledge. In their analysis, the "racialized, gendered, and ethnocentric" bent of "Western" philosophy, which developed out of the particular experiences of a privileged male few, can be traced back to the role of a philosopher in these knowledgemaking processes (Outlaw 1998: 389). A select few used their own particular experiences as a universal standard for humanity. What philosophically sound reasons, then, they ask, justify the prolonged use of this standard self-understanding today? None at all.

Such critiques are supplemented by the work of other colleagues who strive to make the "unplumbed philosophical riches" of other philosophical traditions available to us (Berger 2015: 11). Some such studies refrain from using a conceptual lens familiar to us, and exogenous to the context in question. They endeavor to make a context meaningful by capturing all salient moments immanent to it. These studies underscore that world philosophies are not mere, premodern historic relics. They can be rich conceptual resources for us only if we find adequate ways to relate to them and make meaning of them for our own lives. As we see, varied attempts around the world aspire to halt the "hegemony in the production of theories" where one part of the world only serves as "'objects' of study in discursive systems originating from" elsewhere (Dalmiya 2016: 302).

Conclusion: Moving Forward

In sum, postwar comparative philosophy began as a laudable venture. Faced by the moral catastrophe of colonialism and the Holocaust, its practitioners dared to dream of a peaceful world. The work comparative philosophy enabled over the last few decades, however, has laid bare the limited applicability of this approach to our world. Neither the vision of a monolithic world-order nor the binaries emanating from it give us appropriate tools to make sense of our interconnected postcolonial world. Rather, our age—what Jonardon Ganeri calls the "age of re:emergence"—demands us to conceptualize a decidedly open understanding of philosophy, which is not subservient to dominant paradigms in the field (2016: 137). The world-philosophies approach seeks to develop precisely such an open-ended view on philosophies of the world. Importantly, it does not claim to develop one right theory which then can be applied to practice. Rather, it chooses to pay attention to "how its framing network of concepts renders objects or events in the world as intelligible for inquiry" (Kim 2019: 45).

Through its commitment to plurality, this approach explicitly distances itself from a center-periphery framework, in which only one single center bestows upon itself the power to map the philosophical terrain for different locales on the periphery. Concomitantly, it rejects the binary on the temporal axis too, which bifurcates a static, premodern past from a progressive, modern present. Rather, the world-philosophies approach deliberately focuses on the temporal intersection and divergence between the past, present, and future. It deliberately makes room for a creative and critical reappropriation of the past in such a way that this rearticulation enables one to make sense of lived experiences here and now. To enable such a recontextualization, it homes in on "subversive interplays between a plurality of open vernaculars and new, non-coercive, ways to think about our common humanity" (Ganeri 2016: 138).

Chapter Overview

Chapter 2 will provide an introductory overview of the narrative that takes us from the multicultural histories of philosophy of the early modern period to the staunchly eurocentric discipline of philosophy as we find it today. Recent scholarship suggests that the current accepted narrative of the history of philosophy—that is, one beginning with the Greeks and culminating in Europe in the modern period—took root in European discourses only in the eighteenth century, under the influence of an emerging pseudoscience of race (cf. Park 2013). As the chapter discusses, Kant's contentious view on racial essentialism, which undergirds his work on the history of philosophy, forms the historical backdrop against which philosophy departments in most of the world's regions are shaped even today.

To adequately address this inheritance of dubious historical narratives requires some discussion of the historical development of disciplinary categories in academia. Taking the examples of "religion" and "philosophy," this chapter will look in more detail at the history of the translation of these terms into Japanese during the colonial period. Such examples concretely illustrate how the Kantian-Hegelian legacy prevalent in philosophy can be resisted. The next three chapters will flesh out this chapter's larger claim that a more critical, creative, and speculative approach to the study of world philosophies is warranted if we seek to resist this legacy. This chapter, as with all the chapters in the book, ends with a list of topics for further discussion. The final sections of the book include "Teaching Notes" and "Teaching Suggestions" for classroom activities and assignments. These sections provide further guidance for those who might wish to assign this book itself, or parts of it, to students.

Chapter 3 begins our discussion of the book's central concern with selves, worlds, and ways of knowing. The third chapter looks to recent work in cross-cultural feminist theory and philosophy of race to underscore one of our major claims that knowledge making is a relational endeavor, which is to say, it is constituted by and within an interpersonal and environmental context. This critique illustrates why the conventional notion of a transcendental, unified, and universal knowing self should be reconsidered. Leaning on insights from this work, we first develop the notion of a relational self. We then proceed to analyze how rethinking the distinction between "knowing that" and "knowing how," along the lines suggested by Linda Martín Alcoff and Vrinda Dalmiya, can be advantageous to the study of world philosophies. Inasmuch as this rethinking puts the spotlight on people and not on specific outcomes of their mental processes, this rethinking brings into focus the need to be more attentive to the power dynamics involved in the act of knowing. This attentiveness allows a learner, a knower, or a teacher to consciously work on herself to develop mindful techniques that can offset the power dynamics that unfold in processes of knowing. As an illustrative example of the world-philosophical approach in action, we draw on insights from *qi*-based philosophies to make sense of the claim that we do not live our lives within our skins. This chapter, as well as next two that follow, includes an extended section titled "In the Classroom," where we discuss in detail syllabus modules and pedagogical strategies we have used in our own classes while covering this material with students. In this case, we discuss the use of pedagogies internal to Chinese philosophical traditions, including the memorization of core texts, contemplative reading practices, and commentarial writing as a form of philosophical expression.

Chapter 4 will engage the interconnection between a relational knower and the world. This chapter will address the following questions: if a relational knower seeks to approach the classification of content with an eye toward the terms and categories indigenous to the source material, how then would this knower navigate through the conventional use of terms like "Chinese philosophy," "Japanese philosophy," "African philosophy," and so on? As we will see, the notion of a relational knower helps to us to make methodological choices in the use of terms appropriate for teaching world philosophies.

As another illustrative example of the world-philosophical approach, these methodological ruminations form the backdrop against which the rich debate on the African notion of personhood is analyzed. This example is salient for several reasons: for one, it shows that a clear-cut distinction between the self and the world cannot be maintained in some philosophical traditions. To know the self is to know how to become one's self in a larger social world. This part of the discussion complements the insights of Chapter 3. In addition, the debate on African personhood is useful in shedding light on the difficulties—and advantages—associated with the continued use of the term "philosophy" in other cultural traditions as well as the dilemmas raised by the use of the qualifier "African" in this context. For this chapter's section on issues "In the Classroom," we cite our experiences with co-teaching as a pedagogical strategy for resisting the marginalization of Indigenous philosophies in academia.

Chapter 5 follows the relational knower into two additional worlds of philosophy: the worlds of philosophy in the Islamic and Indic contexts. We will study in detail with these examples how the relational knower encourages us to depart from the standard renditions of such philosophies. Conventional textbook accounts on philosophy in the Islamic world seem to be in general driven by a strict distinction between actors who worked to shape the inheritance of a tradition and scholars working to represent it. Their counterparts on Indic traditions seem to presume that the *darsanic* traditions of Sanskritic India can be safely relegated to intellectual history. In such a framing of both these traditions, they are, albeit in different ways, said to be superfluous to the intellectual pursuits of moderns like us. They may be studied in disciplines like religious studies, area studies, even history; but their philosophical significance to us is negligible. By following the relational knower into such worlds, we see that this standard way of presenting such traditions is implausible. In fact, such a demarcation of philosophy from non-philosophy not only echoes certain events in the history of Europe. It also attests to the gate-keeping practices prevalent in the discipline today, which ensure that this demarcation is sustained.

The chapter illustrates how an engagement with thinkers and positions from world philosophies has the potential to help us make sense of our presentist concerns more fully. To do so however, it suggests that we should not rest content with the way we learn and teach world philosophies. We should not abide by the standard belief that professional philosophers can indeed live within their own skins. To underscore this point, this chapter's section "In the Classroom" reviews an activity that invites students to work alongside us in addressing the dilemmas surrounding the construction of philosophy as an academic discipline at the structural level, by asking them to design a "dream department" informed by a world-philosophical approach.

Chapter 6 will offer a brief summary of the book's reflections. Here, we will revisit our reasons for working with the model of a relational knower to engage selves, worlds, and ways of knowledge production for a judicious teaching of world philosophies. Our approach to world philosophies is an invitation to join in the ongoing conversation about diverse philosophies from myriad perspectives. To borrow Souleymane Bachir Diagne's words, we encourage readers and series' authors to lift "one's eyes to the book of the world" (2018: 75). Different routes lead to different worlds of philosophy; the path struck by this book is merely one of the many.

Discussion Questions

- What does it mean to say that philosophy is an "ever-present human possibility"?
- Find examples from other philosophy classes to illustrate that philosophy is organically linked up with the concrete conditions of existence, such as historical context, sociopolitical context, and

cultural context. Can you make a case for the study of world philosophies using these examples?

- How might philosophers attempt to rein in binary thinking regarding cultural differences, such as the presumed differences between "East" and "West"? What associations do we, or our students, already bring to these words? What strategies might we take to complicate our understanding of cultural difference?
- What are the larger ramifications of the Māori view that everything, every single activity, arises from an act of creation? How does this contrast with a so-called scientific worldview? What presuppositions do we already bring to our understanding of the "scientific worldview"? How do certain presuppositions about science and rationality relate to dominant models for philosophical practice in the Euro-American context?

2

World Philosophies in Historical Perspective

If we survey the various histories of philosophy written in Europe between the 1500s and 1800s, we will find over twenty that either attribute the origins of philosophy to a non-Greek source (such as Egypt or India) or which survey multiple philosophical traditions originating in different areas, including (to name just a few) Persia, Ethiopia, China, and, in one case, Canada (by which the author meant the indigenous peoples of the Americas) (Park 2013: 70–7). As this shows, a polycentric view of philosophy used to be the norm; or, in other words, European scholars were once treating all philosophies as "world philosophies" without needing to name this as such.

However, if we look at philosophy as a discipline today, we find a different picture: introductory textbooks routinely specify the Greeks as the unique originators of philosophy; the philosophical historical narrative generally runs from the pre-Socratics, to Europe's modern period, and onto the development of the analytic-continental divide; and the study of "world philosophies" has become a special topic relegated to elective courses or perhaps the occasional egalitarian "intro to philosophy" survey class. What accounts for this change? The exclusion of non-European thinkers and texts from the canon of philosophy occurred alongside the pseudoscientific theorization of "race" as a biological category in the eighteenth and nineteenth centuries. Or, as explained below, the Greeks became the unique originators of philosophy around the same time that they became "white." This chapter provides an introductory overview of the narrative that takes us from the multicultural histories of philosophy of the early modern period to the staunchly eurocentric discipline of philosophy as we find it today.

Racism and the Development of Academic Philosophy in the Eighteenth Century

The main author of the philosophical canon and historical narrative that we have inherited is the well-known Enlightenment thinker Immanuel Kant (1724–1804). Philosophers including Emmanuel Chukwudi Eze and Robert Bernasconi have long argued that Kant's views on racial essentialism inform his philosophical theories in many ways, but especially in his construction of the history of philosophy (Eze 1997; Bernasconi 2003). More recently, the intellectual historian Peter K. J. Park has provided careful and thorough historical evidence of this claim. As Park asks, "Was Kant a racial thinker? According to Bernasconi, he was one of the founding theorists of race. Was Kant a racist? A first-time reader of 'Observations on the Feeling of the Beautiful and the Sublime' may well be shocked and disturbed by Kant's racial stereotypes and racist remarks" (2013: 93). Park elaborates that these statements include Kant's conviction that no African person has ever made any artistic or scientific achievements, and that black skin color is proof of stupidity. According to the theories of racial essentialism that inform Kant's anthropology, the relative achievements of the different races reflect their respective abilities and limitations:

> Kant taught that the Hindu race did not develop philosophy because they did not have that capacity. In his anthropology lectures, Kant explicitly attributes this lack *not* to the form of government or customs of the Asians, but to their descent (*Abstammung*). Montesquieu had

> famously argued that the form of government or customs of a people determined its character. Kant taught his students that it was the other way around. It is race that determines the form of government and the customs. (2013: 94)

In other words, for Kant, "white" Europeans are the only people who developed philosophy, whereas "black," "yellow," and "red" people did not, because of their inherent characteristics as members of different races.

Moreover, as Park's work makes clear, philosophers today should not assume that Kant was simply a product of his time, that is, that he absorbed a racist worldview from prevailing currents. To the contrary, theories of race were debated, being divided among a range of positions, some quite egalitarian. From out of this spectrum, Kant chose to advance a contentious theory of racial essentialism, promoted by three specific figures: the historians Christoph Meiners (1747–1810) and Wilhelm Gottfried Tenneman (1761–1819), and the physiologist Friedrich Tiedemann (1781–1861). The core thesis of Park's book is that Kant's view on racial essentialism undergirds his work on the history of philosophy—it informs Kant's arguments for the exclusion of African and Asian sources from the canon and his insistence that philosophy flowered spontaneously among the Greeks with no influence from outside the Greek-speaking world. Again, as Park stresses, Kant was here advancing what we might call a fringe view, which was not representative of the diversity of opinions on philosophy's history available to Kant at that time.

In fact, as Park goes on to say: "That philosophy was exclusively of Greek origin was an opinion held by only three published historians of philosophy in the eighteenth century"—namely, the same Meiners, Tiedemann, and Tenneman whose theories so influenced Kant's anthropology (2013: 8). So, Park's research allows us to make the claim, fairly confidently, that the Greeks enjoy the status they have today largely because they were appropriated in the late 1700s into the racist narrative of world-historical development promoted by a small subset of scholars at the time. This fringe view went on to influence the Kantian School and eventually to assume a dominant position within academia, such that today's philosophy departments are the inheritors of a historical narrative and a textual canon shaped by the dubious racial theories of a handful of eighteenth-century Europeans.

Racism and Philosophy Today

With the use of the standard canon, Kant's limited view on philosophy's history has been successfully exported around the globe. At universities worldwide, philosophy professors are expected to fall into either "continental" or "analytic" camps, meaning that they work mainly in the philosophy of continental Europe or mainly in the philosophy of the Anglophone lineage. Their departments rely on the same canon and historical narrative that is mainstream in the United States. For example, at the major universities of China and Japan, you will find Buddhist scholarship taking place not in the philosophy departments but in places such as "religious studies" or "area studies." Addressing this phenomenon requires some discussion of the historical development of disciplinary categories in academia today, especially as these inform the disciplinary agendas that our *Bloomsbury Introductions to World Philosophies* seeks to disrupt.

For example, for the purposes of the *Bloomsbury Introductions*, when we speak of "Buddhist scholarship" in the context of world philosophies, we do not mean "scholarship about Buddhism" as might be conducted by an anthropologist or a historian. We mean, instead, the rich history of Buddhist philosophical inquiry as exemplified, perhaps, by the famed monastic university of Nālandā, which operated in India from approximately the fifth to the thirteenth centuries and attracted students from Korea to Indonesia. We might say that Nālandā is, indeed, a pivotal institution in the history of world philosophies, in that it trained several of the most influential translators of Sanskrit texts into Chinese, including Xuanzang (602–664) and Yijing (635–713). The scholarly traditions of Nālandā persist to this day at the Buddhist universities of Tibet, with the current Dalai Lama considering himself a member of the Nālandā lineage (Dalai Lama et al. 2011: 15–16).

Several contemporary Buddhist philosophers from America and Europe have studied at these Tibetan universities as scholars and, for some, as Buddhist practitioners. Many are products of the Emory-Tibet Partnership program housed in the Department of Religion at Emory University (USA).[1] There, faculty members include both Euro-American-trained PhD holders and Tibetan-trained *geshe*, the academic degree of the Tibetan monastic system. Other European and American Buddhist philosophers have been trained at the University of Chicago's prestigious School of Divinity,[2] where specialists in Buddhism are affiliated with the school's internal programs in Philosophy of Religion and History of Religion as well as the university's Department of South Asian Languages and Civilizations, Department of East Asian Languages and Civilizations, Department of Art History, and other departments in the humanities and social sciences. No specialists in Buddhism are affiliated with the Department of Philosophy at Chicago at the time of this writing. This general pattern is typical across the United States, and, as said earlier, across the globe. Indeed, only two PhD-granting philosophy departments in the United States regularly employ Buddhist philosophers—the University of New Mexico,[3] a center for South Asian Buddhist thought, and the University of Hawaiʻi at Mānoa,[4] which maintains specialists in Indian, Chinese, and Japanese traditions.

The fact that most Buddhist philosophy globally today takes place in religion departments has to do with the contested categories of philosophy, religion, and science in the history of European thought.

As Jason Josephson-Storm has demonstrated, the word "religion" has traveled across cultures not alone but as a part of a larger conceptual apparatus.[5] In the essay "The Superstition, Secularism, and Religion Trinary" (2018), he argues that the under-theorized category of "superstition" serves to police the boundaries of both religion "proper" and the assumed rational character of secular, scientific inquiry. We might add that "philosophy" as a discipline has been caught up in this same convoluted conceptual web.

For example, a central point of tension is made visible when we ask whether "religion" is aligned with reason or with superstition. As is well known, European colonization was framed as a civilizing mission, which involved bestowing a key civilizational marker—that is, religion—to those presumed lacking in civilization (see Chapter 5). So, when deployed as a vehicle for colonization, the rational and universal aspects of religion are emphasized. From this perspective, there can only be one true religion, that is, Christianity, which is opposed to the superstitions of "paganism." The former is portrayed as a friend to science, progress, and other Enlightenment values; while the latter is depicted as backward, irrational, and even dangerous. However, as the fraught history of the Enlightenment in Europe shows, Christianity itself was often cast as the superstitious element in contrast to the rationality of science, philosophy, and secular humanism. This accounts for G. W. F. Hegel's claim, in *Lectures on the History of Philosophy*, that what "we call Eastern Philosophy is more properly the religious mode of thought" (1995: 117). As such, he counts it as pre-philosophical and includes a discussion of it only to illustrate its difference from the "true Philosophy" that develops later in Greece (1995: 117). The fact that Buddhist philosophy is today located in religion departments is a persistent vestige of this Hegelian ranking of cultures on the world-historical stage.

This erstwhile ranking of cultures continues to tie in well with the standard narrative professional philosophy tells of itself. As its self-image will have it, eurocentric professional philosophy perceives itself as a branch of independent inquiry that has been hugely successful in sundering its ties with ecclesial authority in Europe. This separation could be successfully maintained over the last centuries through the fierce allegiance of its practitioners to the power of reason. Not only did the racialization sketched earlier become invisible in the discipline's self-image, but the geography of philosophical reason, which posits Europe "as the highest manifestation of the purity of reason, and thus of humanity itself" (Monahan 2011: 165), was lost from view, too. In the next chapter, we will study why this self-image merits a closer, critical analysis. Here, it suffices to note that this self-image has come at a high cost for the practice of philosophy. Rather than simply falling in line and accepting this bequeathed narrative, let us see where a departure from some of its signposts would take us.

Philosophy in Translation

To make visible "world philosophies" in a way that resists the Hegelian legacy will require that we bracket our assumptions about the apparent naturalness of generic categories such as "religion" and "philosophy." Toward that end, let us look in more detail at the history of the translation of these terms into non-European languages during the colonial period. The word "religion" derives from a Latin root (*religio*), whose precise meaning is unclear; although, as Josephson-Storm says: "Regardless of its origins, in pre-Christian Roman usage, *religio* generally referred to a prohibition or an obligation" (2012: 17). By the fifteenth century, *religio* was used in Catholicism to refer to "the performance of ritual obligations, especially . . . to describe a state of life bound by monastic vows"; and, accordingly, "the noun 'the religious' referred to monks and nuns" (2012: 16). Strictly speaking, these terms are specific to European intellectual history; or, as Robert Ford Campany says: "Discourse about religions is rooted in Western language communities and in the history of Western cultures. . . . To speak of 'religions' is to demarcate things in ways that are not inevitable or immutable but, rather, are contingent on the shape of Western history, thought, and institutions. Other cultures may, and do, lack closely equivalent demarcations" (2003: 289). By the eighteenth and nineteenth centuries, European scholars had developed a specific way to "demarcate things" with a hierarchical schema that tended to include, according to Tomoko Masuzawa's analysis, Christianity as the one true religion, Judaism and Islam as "almost Christian, or at least would-be Christians" (Masuzawa 2005: 49), and a multitude of so-called idolators or heathens who did not possess true religion at all.

Prior to colonial contact, some other areas of the world demarcated things differently. We focus in what follows on the Japanese context. When Japanese scholars first encountered European cultures and traditions, the Japanese language had no precise equivalents for terms such as "philosophy," "religion," or "science." In other words, these were not the generic categories by which the Japanese would attempt to understand and classify foreign traditions. To the contrary, Japanese discourses were shaped by at least three major categories, including the Chinese "scholarly lineage" (Ch. *rujia* 儒家), the South Asian *dharma* ("teachings") of Śakyamuni Buddha, and, later, the Tokugawa-period "ancient studies" (Jp. *kogaku* 古学) or "national learning" (Jp. *kokugaku* 国学) movements.

By China's "scholarly lineage" we mean the tradition that European languages have come to call "Confucianism," a somewhat misleading term that portrays the historical figure of "Confucius" (Kongzi 孔子, 551–479 BCE) as the founder of some sort of movement. In fact, the tradition known in Chinese as *rujia* (儒家) well predates the life of Kongzi, and Kongzi himself denies being an innovator (*Lunyu* 論語 2011: 3.14).[6] Rather, he was a member of the "lineage" or "family" (*jia* 家) of the *ru* (儒), a term better translated as "scholar" or "literati." The *ru* were members of China's educated elite: they were most often employed as educators or government officials, they were versed in the classic philosophical and literary texts of Chinese culture, and they were qualified to preside over various state rites and civic ceremonies as well as the rituals performed at ancestral shrines. Throughout this book, we use the alternative English terms "Ruism" and "Ruists" to refer to the tradition and its members.

Reflecting the diversity and complexity of the tradition, the Japanese of the Meiji period would have understood Ruism to include studies of ethics, politics, and statecraft; empirical investigations of the natural world (especially astronomy); training in music, poetry, and gymnastics; the maintenance of official court rites and ceremonies; and institutions of family and civic ancestor worship. Similarly, the *buddha-dharma* (Jp. *buppō* 佛法) would have been understood to be multifaceted: it was concerned with existential matters; it inquired into the conditions of life, death, and future rebirths; and, in terms of practice, it was associated with institutions of monasticism, on the one hand, and lay rituals for generating merit, on the other hand. As with Ruism, the Japanese usage of dharma could be applied to diverse schools of thought marked by, at times, radical disagreements over how to interpret and practice basic Buddhist principles.

When the Japanese first encountered Jesuit priests in the mid-1500s, they classified Christianity as a deviant form of dharma and promptly banned it (Josephson 2012: 24–8). As this indicates, dharma was here used as a flexible cross-cultural category—a genus that could plausibly include unfamiliar or foreign species. What difference might it make were we to inquire today into the various dharma of the world, rather into the world's philosophies and religions? What if we still conceived of dharma and Ruism as two separate generic categories rather than as two species of either philosophy or religion? Answers to these questions will remain speculative, since, over time, the indigenous Japanese conceptual framework was eventually overlaid with European terms, which were soon exported to China via the written characters shared by the Japanese and Chinese languages.

Such translation efforts escalated with the Perry Expedition's forceful opening of the Japanese economy to international trade in the mid-1800s. Japan was compelled to sign a number of treaties with American and European governments, all of which included clauses requiring Japan to acknowledge "freedom of religion." As Josephson says:

> When Japanese translators first encountered the English word "religion" in the international trade treatises of the late 1850s, they were perplexed and had difficulty finding the proper corresponding term in Japanese. There was no indigenous word that referred to something as broad as "religion" nor a systematic way to distinguish between "religions" as members of a larger generic category. Instead, words such as *shū* 宗, *kyō* 教, *ha* 派 or *shūmon* 宗門 were used interchangeably to designate Christianity, divisions within Buddhism, distinctions between Daoism and Confucianism, and different strands of intellectual thought (such as different schools of painting or mathematics). . . . Ultimately, some translators chose to render "religion" as "sect law" (*shūhō* 宗法) while others settled on "sect doctrine" (*shūshi* 宗旨). Regardless, both terms were already situated in their own system of meaning, referring generally to a preexisting sub-categorization of Buddhist schools. (2006: 144)

The word that eventually sticks, and which we use today, is *shūkyō* (宗教); like the other words Josephson cites earlier, it has a notably Buddhist flavor. Specifically, *shūkyō* was an obscure compound from Chinese sources that referred to doctrinal differences between different Buddhist sects. This is perhaps a small victory in the colonial context in which these translations were taking place, because the Buddhist-flavored terminology does not fully capitulate to foreign categories; that is, the use of *shūkyō* retains the impression that Christianity, and religion at large, can be categorized in Buddhist terms. That said, in contemporary usage, the Buddhist connotations of *shūkyō* have receded.

The translation of "philosophy" as *tetsugaku* (哲学) shares a related history. The term was coined in 1874 by Nishi Amane (1829–1897). Just as *shūkyō* once had Buddhist connotations, *tetsugaku* "echoes older

Confucian words such as *tetsujin* or sage" (Maraldo 2011: 555). Despite this Ruist heritage, Nishi was clear that his intention was to translate the name of a European discipline that had no precise analogue in either Chinese or Japanese sources (2011: 556). He defined philosophy according to European accounts influential in his time, describing it as the love of wisdom, a discourse on first principles, and the unitary foundation underlying the various sciences (2011: 556–8). The term was given more explicitly Kantian associations by Inoue Enryō (1858–1919) in his 1886 work *An Evening of Philosophical Conversation*. There, he imagines a group of travelers on a boat discussing the meaning of philosophy: "This *tetsugaku* is a new kind of discipline that has come from the West, but just what sort of discipline is it?" Inoue answers:

> There are . . . several disciplines that have to do with matters of the mind: psychology, logic, ethics, and pure *tetsugaku*. People are more or less familiar with psychology, logic, and so forth, but when it comes to pure *tetsugaku* people haven't the slightest idea of what it is. In short, pure *tetsugaku*, as the study of the pure principles of *tetsugaku*, must be called the study that inquires into the axioms of the truth and the foundation of the disciplines. (qtd. in Maraldo 2011: 561)

This notion of "pure *tetsugaku*" (*junsei tetsugaku* 純正哲学) is modelled on the Kantian terms "pure philosophy" (*reine Philosophie*) and pure reason (*reine Vernunft*) (Maraldo 2014: 213). Inoue is obviously excited by what he sees as philosophy's critical and progressive potential, as a discipline that allows for sharp and clear analysis, unbiased judgment, and, perhaps most importantly for Inoue, apprehension of what he called the "absolute" (*zettai* 絶対), which he associated variously with the Hegelian absolute, the Kantian thing-in-itself, and Buddhist "thusness" (Sk. *tathātā*, Jp. *shin'nyo* 真如) (Josephson 2006: 159).[7] Nonetheless, through his work, we witness the historical unfolding of the transmission of a specific, limited, eurocentric version of philosophy to Japan. We could make similar historical studies of the spread of academic philosophy via institutions of higher learning in China, India, Africa, and Latin America, and we would find similar results.

Conclusion: Moving Forward

The *Bloomsbury Introductions to World Philosophies* aims to construct a framework for philosophical diversity that is critical, creative, and speculative. It is critical, in that we remain suspicious as well as skeptical of philosophical norms as we have received them, and we rely heavily on historical critiques in related fields. It is creative and speculative, in that we consciously look beyond eurocentric terms and categories to imagine the practice of philosophy from new perspectives. We do not presume naively to turn back the (colonial) clock, but we do hope to make visible forms of philosophical practice and discourse that have been under-appreciated, or willfully ignored, due to the Kantian-Hegelian legacy outlined in this chapter.

As we have seen in the pages so far, several philosophers today are not content to accept and further propagate the standard narrative of eurocentric academic philosophy. They are concerned about how that which we simply call *philosophy* is deeply saturated with Europeanness, whiteness, and maleness. These philosophers direct their critical attention to bringing to light this particularity so that what Michael Monahan calls the "racialized understanding of rationality" can be corrected (2011: 175). Philosophers like Monahan push back against the "politics of purity" (2011: 219) that continues to be played out in the discipline, not only in Europe but also in large parts of the world.

As mentioned in Chapter 1, we seek to move away from the conventional monological outlook on philosophy, which till today presumes that only one universal framework can adequately capture all the worlds of philosophy on the ground. We refrain from retrospectively projecting an idea of philosophy onto these worlds, which may render past philosophers "Everyman with pocket editions or Internet downloads" (Nylan 2016: 100). Relatedly, we depart from the conventional practice of philosophy that posits the philosopher as a thinker whose thoughts deliver an adequate representation of the objects of inquiry. Rather, we hold that the latter largely depend on the conceptual nets we cast on worlds of philosophy. We reap as we sow. Whether we can make sense of the worlds of philosophy will depend on our conceptual framing and openness to attend to the specificity of differing contexts. When texts were circulated in manuscript cultures, for example, their reach was restricted to select groups, in which one often interacted on a one-to-one basis with the tutor. These texts did not "fix" knowledge in the manner in which they do so today; rather they served as guides in memorization (2016: 92–5). Manuscript cultures abounded in different parts of the world. In noting some main differences to a print book, Peter Barker writes:

> In a manuscript-based culture, commentaries and glosses begin as notes literally written in the margins of the original work. When the work is next copied these may be incorporated into the main manuscript, creating a new book with additional, original content. This process can go on as long as anyone is interested in the book. In other words, a manuscript book is a wiki, but a print book is only a text. (2017: 40)

But what does this mean for the study of world philosophies? We turn to that question in the following chapters.

Discussion Questions

- How does the dominant historical narrative of academic philosophy impact its practice today?
- Would multicultural histories of philosophy change classical philosophical subdisciplines like logic, metaphysics, aesthetics, and ethics?

- Can you pinpoint how the Hegelian ranking of cultures on the world-historical stage becomes visible in the philosophy classes you attend or have attended? What about classes in other departments as well?
- Does translation of philosophical content from one language to another entail some loss in content? Can you anticipate what would be lost in translation?

3

Relational Knowing, Self-Making, and the Study of World Philosophies

As mentioned in Chapter 2, our volume aims to construct a framework for philosophical diversity that is critical, creative, and speculative. So, how could one deploy this framework such that it can track diversity? The following chapters will follow this trail. But why is a notion as "philosophical diversity" needed at all? What considerations prompt it? Let us turn to this aspect first before examining how relational knowing can contribute to tracking philosophical diversity in a critical and creative way.

Moving Away from a Conventional Understanding of the Knower

As one hitherto dominant understanding of philosophy will have it, professional philosophy is engaged in "disinterested," "impartial," and "neutral" inquiry into the very essence of our being. Disinterested, impartial, and neutral results are said to be achieved through a separation between oneself and the world in the act of knowing. Crucial to this separation is the view that philosophical inquiry is driven by an ahistorical, culturally invariant, unified, and universal self. Regardless of the spatiotemporal location in which philosophical inquiry takes place, this self is able to achieve the same culturally invariant results.

Work in feminist theory and critical race studies provides reasons to doubt this view. Let us begin with the complex character of human understanding as well as knowing. When we seek to understand something, we do not encounter phenomena as entities or facts external to us. At any point in time, we are deeply intertwined with the world even as we attempt to understand it. As such, understanding is a process with a strong social dimension. But this is not all.

Several social factors seep into our philosophical inquiry. They influence our processes of understanding deeply. The knowable world is not external to the relations of knowing. In fact, we gather information through these relations and know through them too. Our knowledge-seeking endeavor depends upon such relations. It is particular through and through. The questions we seek to ask in philosophical inquiry, and the answers we claim to obtain in this process, are deeply colored by our social relations. Our social class, gender, ethnicity, age, cultural affiliation, linguistic capacities, and so on intersect in complex ways when we seek to understand the world. Importantly, these are not impediments to good philosophy but integral to self-aware and self-critical epistemic practice. But if understanding (and concomitantly knowing) are social processes, why does philosophical inquiry conventionally hold that the knowing self can and should be abstracted from the world or from historical and cultural context?

Like any other social activity, philosophical knowledge is generated in specific socio-material and temporal settings. Human beings have better chances of understanding the world around them when they team up with others to gather information about it. Knowledge is made, that is, tested, transmitted, and modified within this specific community through the information group members share with each other. However, in generating knowledge for its own members, such a bounded community may engage in exclusionary practices. We suggest that academic norms in philosophy today are exclusionary precisely because eurocentric philosophy has not been challenged to reflect on its own cultural milieu or engage across cultures.

Take trust attribution within a given community, for example. It is sometimes easier to locate reliable, trustworthy sources of information solely within one's own group. One would not need to explain basic background assumptions to other group members, nor would a sizeable majority be likely to hold totally opposing views.

A good example of such an assumption would be the aforementioned separation between a knower and the world. Fielded within a relatively homogenous community of knowers, it may not be contested by a single member within the group. Were a member to problematize what from the inside may seem to be an innocuous presumption, the community may foreclose further inquiry into it, especially when its discursive practices are not geared to engage seriously with metatheoretical issues. This could be one of the reasons why historical practices of trust attribution within academic philosophy have yet to be faced squarely.

As we know today, academic philosophy was conducted predominantly by a group of white, male, propertied philosophers in Europe and later in North America. This relatively homogenous demographic makeup did not, it seems, sufficiently motivate them to carefully study how experiential subjectivity and objective social factors crisscross in multiple complex ways, or to engage with what Charles Mills calls the "normative dimension of epistemology" (1988: 251). One result of this homogeneity was clear: "Those who know what knowing is quickly became those—and only those—who could know *fully*" (Outlaw 1996: 56). These historical patterns of exclusionary trust attribution continue to cast their shadow on the profession today. It remains exclusionist.[1] As such, academic philosophy in the aforementioned countries continues to be predominantly white and "stereotyped as male" (Beebee and Saul 2011: 7).

Now, if erstwhile exclusionary practices of making philosophical knowledge have been continued, these practices may remain insufficiently attentive to the downside of group homogeneity, too. But as recent research highlights, members of homogenous knowledge communities tend to overestimate their own performance. They often perceive themselves as being more effective and are more confident about their problem-solving abilities than heterogenous groups (cf. Bruya 2017: 999).

Let us pause for a moment. What is the upshot of our discussion for the study of world philosophies? There is reason to assume that current ways of making philosophical knowledge reinforce the group's homogeneity. These may be directly feeding into the belief that eurocentric philosophy is, in general, the only viable philosophy under the sun. As a result, "there are whole territories of *philosophy* most have never explored" (Olberding 2017: 1035). How, then; can we even begin to make a case for an exploration of those unexplored territories of philosophy? One way would be to revise the notion of the knowing self. It could perhaps be recalibrated such that it would, at a minimum, make the knower more sensitive to her own imbrication in social contexts. Can the notion of relational knowing deliver in this regard? Let us see.

Relational Knowing and Social Contexts

As we saw earlier, knowing is a social process. Our being in the world heavily influences our knowing the world. The standard philosophical notion of an unchanged knower is in sharp contrast to how we actually obtain information about the world. In the process of obtaining information, we seem to travel across varied contexts. Several epistemic shifts and somersaults facilitate our information-obtaining practices. Precisely these shifts give us a foothold into understanding the specificities of these contexts. Being connected with, and imbricated in, the phenomena in the world, the knowing self is in constant flux. It gains in depth through its engagement with the world. Yet, a sense of self is generated through the temporal continuity of its experiences as well as, to use Mariana Ortega's term, through an attribution of "mineness" (2016: 80).

Even if one were to concede that the knowing self is in flux, how should this in any manner impact that which is known? After all, that which is known seems to remain true despite the various contexts in which it is instantiated. Should its status as truth be dubitable right from the start, we might have to consider whether it deserves to be called truth and thus justifiably be regarded as a knowledge claim.

In their article, "Are 'Old Wives' Tales' Justified," Linda Martín Alcoff and Vrinda Dalmiya (1993) problematize this very practice of identifying philosophical truth. The standard view divides up our world by clearly demarcating a realm of knowledge from that of non-knowledge. The former is said to be constituted by propositions that adhere to the "*S* knows that *p*" model. The standard view sets this realm in contrast to another domain, which in general is considered to be irrelevant for philosophical knowledge. This is the realm of "knowing how."

Martín Alcoff and Dalmiya (1993: 232) take on what the philosopher Gilbert Ryle called the "intellectualist legend" head on. They focus on the viability of one important presumption underlying the standard view, according to which "propositions are considered to be intersubjectively available to all subjects" inasmuch as they are expressed in a neutral language, which is accessible to all participants (1993: 230). But is this really the case? Not only is the language used in philosophical discourse not neutral, but also its non-neutrality may just hinder it from tracking other genuinely cognitive activities. If that is the case, the current demarcation between knowledge and non-knowledge may be arbitrary. Furthermore, it may also be unreasonably discrediting other ways in which we know and navigate around our world.

For Martín Alcoff and Dalmiya, the epistemic significance of both the activities involved in knowing is undeniable: "Knowing is not necessarily a matter of saying and representing what is the case but can also be a practical involvement with the world" (1993: 235). Both aspects are needed to be in the world. In addition, they illustrate that propositions are generated even when we attempt to know how to *do* something. A person may have a "nascent grasp of the rules and principles underlying her activity that enable her to 'recognize' a clear formulation of them, and it is the latter that makes her simple skill *cognitively* relevant" (1993: 236–7). And yet, the distinction between knowing that and knowing how does not have to be abandoned completely. The former may be characterized by a distinctive "epistemic attitude" that is not necessarily found in the latter. Martín Alcoff's and Dalmiya's clarifications help in disrupting what María Lugones and Elizabeth Spelman in their influential essay "Have We Got a Theory for You!" call the conventional "hierarchical distinctions between theorizers and those theorized about and between theorizers and doers" (1983: 577).

To relate these ruminations to our context, a sole focus on the knowing-that dimension may mislead a philosopher into believing that the primary purpose of philosophy is to amass supposedly neutral as well as impartial, propositional knowledge about a particular world philosophy. Guided by this belief, one may for this purpose mine other philosophical traditions for analogies to the dominant tradition. Martín Alcoff and Dalmiya deliver good epistemic grounds as to why this narrow view of knowing must be abandoned for a more sustained engagement with other forms of knowing: "Incorporating these substantially distinct forms of knowing into epistemology increases the complexity of our notion of the epistemic and the cognitive" (1993: 241). But there is more. By focusing on the knowing-how dimension as a dimension of epistemic relevance, they also propose that we "make *knowing people* the paradigm of knowledge rather than the knowing of middle-sized physical objects" (Dalmiya 2016: 13). This call for a methodological reset would have consequences for the manner in which knowledge about world philosophies is made.

Let us charitably presume that the knowing-that dimension, all things considered, will be able to generate a roughly adequate description of a physical object. But matters seem to get more complicated when we are dealing with other persons. It is doubtful whether our own subjective description of another person can be reliable and accurate. Should this indeed be the case, it seems that we need to adequately engage with all those characteristics that make her what she is. In this respect, some factors like "features of a subject's mood," "emotional and intellectual character, as well as his [or her] material, historical, and cultural context" seem to be of crucial importance (Creller 2018: 54). Notice though that these factors can change depending on the circumstances. As a result, our knowing the other person seems to be subject to changes in individual factors that feed into this act of knowing, too. But why should "embodied aspects of experience" (2018: 63) change only in the person we seek to know? They could also change in the knower. Ortega tries to capture the dynamism of such processes by highlighting the epistemic shifts necessitated by one's travels in different worlds. These shifts could lead the knower to experience herself as a multiplicitous self, whose sense of being a unified seamless whole is disrupted in everyday interactions. These ruptures could generate a sense of unease, which prompt the knower to reflect more about her own place in the world (2016: 60).

Taken together, the call for a sustained engagement with other forms of knowing, for making people the center of knowledge making, and for a sustained attentiveness to disruptions in one's sense of self could be read as a call to be attentive to power dynamics playing out in the field, too. But are there reasons specific to our context of inquiry that would prod us to focus on power dynamics in knowing relationally?

Power Dynamics in Relational Knowing

Professional philosophers stand in different relations to world philosophies. Some may be associated with them due to their specialization; others may stand in a relation to them on virtue of descent.

Yet others may be related to them through descent and specialization. Despite these differences, there seems to be one common factor across these groups: their (first) training in eurocentric philosophy. They are part of the network that holds professional philosophy together. Due to these intersecting factors, an easy binary between "us, the oppressed" and "them, the oppressors" cannot be sustained in all cases.

Sometimes, a person could find herself in a role associated with erstwhile oppressors, while in other situations the inhabited role could be associated with those of erstwhile oppressed, or even one associated with those who consciously resist oppression. Consequently, oppressors, oppressed, and resisters are not fixed, static points in the role-landscape of professional philosophy. Seeking to capture this momentum, Ortega writes: "Selves need to be understood in their complexity and in terms of the different roles they play in the matrix of power relations such that each of us can be understood variously as oppressors, oppressed, or as resisting" (2016: 51). One may experience an imbalance of power while inhabiting a particular role, while not experiencing it when one switches to another role. "Margins are relative depending on where we plot the center," as Dalmiya puts it pithily (2016: 162).

One possible way to correct this imbalance would be to cultivate relational humility in the act of knowing. This measure would seek to make space for the other person in this act. Such a space could be created by withholding one's biases and expectations, for example. Hereby, a backgrounding of the knowing self and a foregrounding of the other person could be useful. This deliberate act of epistemic self-receding could be deployed by, for example, ascribing ignorance to one's own self and ascribing knowledge to the other person involved in the act of knowing. Through such an "epistemic decentering" of one's own self, one would be better able to center "the epistemic agency of others" (2016: 119).

As Helen Verran argues, foregrounding the agency of other knowers becomes particularly relevant when engaging with members of knowledge traditions that have been hitherto excluded from conventional knowledge frameworks. Verran uses the example of an encounter between a senior environmental scientist and a Yolŋgu Aboriginal landowner in Australia's Dhimirru Indigenous Protected Area to make her point. As she narrates, this scientist asked the fire maker whether two sticks used in firing practices came from the same plant. The answer was positive. In fact, they were said to stand in a grandparent-grandchild relation. This way of classifying the plants contradicted how the scientist had learned to classify them. Instead of confronting the Indigenous knower with this difference head on, the scientist was careful to respond: "I suggested that they were like a man and a woman, the same but different, and he agreed with this analogy" (qtd. in Verran 2013: 144).

Verran concedes that the scientist was indeed trying to be respectful in this encounter. However, instead of allowing himself to squarely face his own "epistemic disconcertment," he polished it over by using an allegory familiar to him. Not only is the use of his particular allegory telling, but the "impetus towards invention and change that can come from a sharply felt encounter with difference" is diffused and/or trapped too (2013: 144). With the use of a naïve allegory, the space, which the scientist had attempted to create for the Indigenous knower at least until the use of the allegory, was inadvertently foreclosed by him. What if, instead, the scientist had seriously considered the meaning of the "grandparent-grandchild" relation and had allowed this indigenous taxonomic model to influence his own understanding of the plants in question? What if he had allowed it to influence his very understanding of "plants"? This would have fostered a more transformative exchange across cultures than the one that actually transpired.

Verran proposes that we seek such transformative encounters for deliberate pedagogical self-reflection. We should allow for moments in which stark epistemic difference is experienced in such encounters. Through these moments, we can bodily experience the "insidious tentacles of the institutions and unacknowledged beliefs within which we negotiate our existential positioning as knowers" (2013: 145). Only when our sense of "epistemic rightness" is rent asunder in these moments, only when we cannot overlook the fissures in our own belief system anymore, can we become sensitized to the overreach of our intellectual habits in shaping our world as knowers. If we, she continues, sincerely seek to make postcolonial knowledge,[2] we must practice an epistemic self-receding such that we learn "to refuse the step which requires a colonising reduction to a shared category, and acceptance, that we may not be metaphysically committed to a common world" (2013: 144). Verran's insights in this regard resonate with James Tully's observation that knowledge about being in the world cannot be developed through a "power-over" but only through "power-with" others (2014: 321).

Cultivating relational humility in knowing practices merits more thought about structural issues though. We know through relations. But as we have seen, several social factors seep into and influence the act of knowing. Knowledge is created through, and within, social and institutional structures. It is implausible to claim that it can arise and be sustained outside these structures. As Leigh Jenco points out: "There is only thought at specific places and times which is subject to institutionalized influence, linguistic dominance, cultural privilege, and other forms of social life seemingly unrelated to knowledge per se" (2016: 285).

Indigenous philosophers Gina Starblanket and Heidi Kiiwetinepinesiik Stark push for a stronger focus on these very structures. They analyze how Indigenous women are portrayed in scholarship (and not only there) as "keepers of relationships" (2018: 185). Such a portrayal assigns to them the role of maintaining healthy relationships. Yet, "the patriarchal nature of the academy" does not give these women the resources to publicly deliberate about what it means to have healthy relationships. Indigenous women's analyses of these relationships continue to be "read more cautiously" than that of their male peers (2018: 187). Given the current imbalance of power in the academy, Starblanket and Stark advocate more critical awareness in engaging with these situations. In their view, this awareness would "reveal and remain mindful of the potential for essentialist or bounded constructions of gender" when it comes to "gender-based constructions of Indigeneity" (2018: 184).

In a similar vein, Bolivian thinker Silvia Rivera Cusicanqui calls for a "decolonization of our gestures and acts and the language with which we name the world" (2012: 105–6). Cusicanqui too warns about the marginalization of Indigenous communities and non-male scholars in the current "economy of ideas" (2012: 103). This economy, Cusicanqui states, tends to favor those specialists whose scholarship will not starkly depart from extant practices of the academy. In the case of Indigenous communities, for example, these specialists tend to continue the extant narrative about them: "A discussion of these communities situated in the 'origin' denies the contemporaneity of these populations and excludes them from the struggles of modernity. They are given a residual status that, in fact, converts them into minorities, ensnaring them in indigenist stereotypes of the noble savage and guardians of nature" (2012: 99).

These interventions are useful in flagging structural issues in our context. Take the university itself. Currently, the demographic makeup of professional philosophy in North America and Europe is not representative of the population. Males and whites tend to be overrepresented, although representative data on the demographic makeup of philosophers in relevant subdisciplines is still lacking. It can be reasonably assumed that male and/or white specialists in world philosophies may be regarded by their peers as an "authenticating presence" (Martín Alcoff 1995: 99) of the tradition in question, although they may not necessarily be representative of the groups they represent. (Donahue's intervention sketched briefly in Chapter 1 has already alerted us to the problematic underside of this representation.) In practicing relational humility in academic spaces, we cannot blanket out this demographic background. We need to be critical in our knowing in order not to reify what we learn through these encounters in academic spaces.

Furthermore, in practicing relational humility mindfully, we may have to be open to the possibility that locales of knowledge making may indeed shift. Placing people in the center of knowledge making does not necessarily entail that knowledge must be sought, and made, solely *outside* academic spaces. Relational knowing can equally take place *within* academic spaces—especially when these are opened up to include those who, for different reasons, do not easily conform to the standard understanding of what it means to be a philosopher. The Indigenous scholars referenced earlier, for example, seek out the academy as at least one site in which knowledge can be reconfigured. Starblanket and Stark, as we saw, make a case for Indigenous representation in the academy, especially of those who do not merely strive to "continue the *transmission* of Indigenous knowledge but also ensure [its] *production*" (2018: 191; emphasis in original). This reconfiguration would, in their estimation, allow Indigenous communities to perceive the continuity of their worldviews and traditions across the temporal frame. Only then can an "Indigenous modernity" (Cusicanqui 2012) emerge.

In knowing relationally, we cannot, thus, abstract from power dynamics that play out in the act of knowing. In fact, facing them squarely enables us to become more attentive to the inertia that our intellectual habits can induce. This inertia can be undercut, as we have learnt from Verran, by *doing difference*. We must be attuned to the sense of unease the experience of difference initiates and implement its pedagogical potential. Arguably, doing difference in this manner would have implications for the way we work on world philosophies. It would need to be stabilized across time too. Let us briefly turn to these points.

Pluralizing Methodologies through Relational Knowing

Relational knowing confronts us with undeniable ambiguities. Admitting this ambiguity neither resigns us to relativism nor renders careful and informed deliberation impossible. Ideally, the sense of unease caused by epistemic disconcertment would shake off the fetters of our mental inertia and bring us to rethink standard practices of knowing. But what would some ensuing pedagogical moments possibly look like? This disconcertment could lead one to pluralize methodologies. In an influential text with the title "On Relativism," Henry Rosemont, Jr. (1988) underscores how a whole barrage of cultural assumptions like beliefs, attitudes, intentions, and so on influence the translation and interpretation of sources from world philosophies. To deal with the source material judiciously, Rosemont proposes that we map these assumptions in the form of a "concept-cluster." The idea is twofold: This mapping would enable us to become more aware about how a whole cluster of concepts work in the background when we translate and interpret. It would, equally, hold us back from making unidimensional one-to-one translations into our own language, and being satisfied with the results.

Rosemont provides an easy example to substantiate the need for work with concept-clusters. Classical Chinese used by Ruist authors did not have a lexical item for "moral." It also lacked corresponding terms for "freedom," "autonomy," "liberty," "rationality," and so on, and also a term for "ought" (1988: 61). Could one take this as evidence to conclude that this tradition lacked a sense of morality? For Rosemont, this would be an implausible, and even irresponsible, conclusion. He appeals to scholars working on world philosophies to develop a methodological sensitivity that would enable them to avoid facile claims like the aforementioned. They should become more aware of the role of "cultural determinants" in the understanding process (1988: 66). Rather than implementing perspectives of our own tradition as hooks into texts from other traditions, he proposes that we ask: "To what extent do these texts suggest that we should be asking very different philosophical questions?" (1988: 66).

Notably, Rosemont's emphasis on methodological sensitivity is not intended to reach an appropriate understanding of (Chinese) sources only. He sees positions incorporated in Chinese source-texts as viable conceptual and practical alternatives to the maladies besetting his own American liberal society. He leans on a Ruist understanding of a role-bearing, relational person to drive the point home that neither we nor any "single culture is already in the possession of [universal] values" (2004: 68).

Jenco strikes a similar tone and takes this position further. She argues that a willingness to distance ourselves from our own methods may enable us to "transform *our* terms of discourse through which *we* operate today and in the future" (2016: 276; emphasis in original). Much like Rosemont, she is optimistic that we can transform ourselves as knowers, both individually and collectively. Jenco's critique is directed toward two groups of postcolonial scholars: the first accepts the eurocentrism permeating our institutions as a pregiven feature of our lives today. This group seems to believe that we should simply accept the ubiquitous, fixed, and static nature of our eurocentric categories. In countering the possible inertia emanating from such a belief, she asks: Why should European thought be "everybody's heritage?" Why do we have to hold on to the belief about the "inescapability of European categories" (2011: 52, 35) when each one of us can work to see what these categories are, namely, local ways of interpreting the world? The second critiqued group consists of scholars who rely solely on European authors, even when they seek to develop theories about decentering the self in knowing processes (2011: 31–3). Jenco rightly warns how this position leads to a dead-end. It inadvertently continues to propagate the belief that theory can be eurocentric only. Universal claims cannot be developed using source material located outside this context. However, the belief in the singular universality of eurocentric theory cannot, as she notes, be backed by historical sources. Continuing to propagate the belief in this universalism would be, to use Martín Alcoff's observation, to "leave intact and unchallenged the geographic imaginary that privileges the West as the origin and principal location of Philosophy" (2017: 403). It would continue the "epistemology of ignorance" prevalent in large parts of the academy (2017: 406).

We have so far sketched two approaches aimed at pluralizing methodological frameworks. Even these cursory sketches suffice to indicate that doing difference could enable a "*finessed*" intermediation between "a totalizing univocity and a complete equivocity" (Morisato 2019: 31). To root our discussion in concrete detail, we next take a more sustained look at methodologies for relational knowing in the Chinese context, following up on the insights offered by Rosemont. The examples from Chinese traditions not only reveal the universalizing aims of Ruist thought but also help underscore the locality and particularity of European and Euro-American ways of knowing the world and navigating through it.

Epistemological Attunement in *Qi*-Based Philosophies

Rosemont and his frequent collaborator Roger Ames have argued that Chinese conceptions of personhood hinge on roles and relationships (e.g., Ames and Rosemont 2016; Ames 2011). As they say: "The starting point is simple. In Confucian role ethics, association is a fact. We do not live our lives inside our skins. Everything we do—physically, psychologically, socially—is resolutely transactional and collaborative" (2016: 12). We want to stress this particular claim that human beings "do not live our lives inside our skins." Ames and Rosemont focus their discussion of role ethics on social and political concerns, but the Ruist conception of relational personhood "outside the skin," as it were, has additional implications for the epistemological issues we have raised so far in this chapter.

We begin with a quote from Joseph Adler on the mind's capacity for knowledge in Ruist thought, which cannot help but sound puzzling without adequate context: "In human beings, spirit [*shen* 神] is a quality of mind—specifically mind-*qi* in its finest, most free-flowing state. . . . To embody this epistemological potential . . . is to be a fully authentic [*cheng*] human being, a Sage" (2004: 141; bracketed material our own). What is "mind-*qi*"? What does it mean to describe a mind as "fine" and "free-flowing"? What is the "epistemological potential" associated with this conception of the mind? In answering these questions, the more radical aspects of our relational knower come to the fore.

The term "*qi*" (氣) refers to the matter-energy matrix of fluid and congealed forces that underlies Ruist sensibilities about the nature of reality, which is to say, the types of things and processes that exist, how they arise, how they interact, and how they can be manipulated. As theorized by the Song (960–1279) and Ming (1368–1644) Ruists, anything that exists is some form of *qi*, whether it is condensed and palpable, as in physical objects, or dispersed and ethereal, as in the spiritual energies of the human mind. We see the impact of this *qi*-based worldview on fields as diverse as medicine, architecture, pedagogy, and cosmology. In most cases, the *qi*-matrix is believed to be structured according to the nested polarities of *yin* (陰) and *yang* (陽), where *yin* refers to forces that settle and sink, that are dark and heavy, and that tend to condense; and *yang* refers to forces that rise or flow, that are clear and light, and that tend to disperse. In these terms, the condensed or coarse *qi* of physical matter is a *yin* force in relation to the *yang* force of the refined and subtle *qi* of human thoughts and sensations. This answers the question of what Adler means when he describes the mind as "fine" and "free-flowing."

Given that *yin-qi* is not categorically different from *yang-qi*, this model admits for a degree of mixing across what dominant philosophical accounts might normally conceive of as the boundary between mind and matter. In the Ruist context, mental experience does not reside only "within our skins," to borrow Ames's and Rosemont's earlier phrase. To the contrary, across an array of philosophical traditions in East Asia (Ruist and Daoist alike[3]), we find the pervasive assumption that mental energies reside both inside and outside the body, that such energies can interact with each other, and that they in turn can interact with other types of energies in the material environment. These various types of energies differ from each other, but not categorically. This is to say that no one phenomenon is what it is inherently but, rather, is what it is dependent on context. These assumptions cannot help but have broad implications for our understanding of the epistemological potential of the relational knower.[4]

Consider, for one example, the famed Song-dynasty philosopher Zhu Xi 朱熹 (1130–1200) and his extensive writings on the nature of the "heart-mind" or of our capacities for "thinking-and-feeling" (*xin* 心). In a detailed study of these writings, the contemporary philosopher Eiho Baba (2017) discusses the mental activity of *zhijue* (知覺). The term is often translated as "perception," having connotations of conscious awareness, intellectual thought, comprehension, and understanding. But, as Baba makes clear, *zhijue* is not simply a faculty of the mind but also an active element in the surrounding environment. Making sense of Zhu Xi's use of this term requires that we put on hold common assumptions about the relationship between the knowing mind and the known world.

As mentioned earlier, subjective sensations and thoughts are classified as types of *yang* energies in relation to the *yin* constitution of the physical body. But within any given *yang-qi* or *yin-qi* phenomenon, there are further *yin* and *yang* aspects. The technical details of Zhu Xi's conception of these nested polarities are important for appreciating what is distinctively relational about his model of the mind. The two forces that Baba highlights in his study of *zhijue* are *hun* (魂) and *po* (魄)—the former is the *yang* process of incorporeal *qi* (i.e., *qi* of the heart-mind) and the latter the *yang* process of corporeal *qi* (i.e., *qi* of the body) (2017: 304). As such, *hun* and *po* refer to the most rarefied or "spiritual" (*shen* 神) aspects of the human heart-mind and body, respectively.

Keeping all this in mind, we can begin to parse the following passage from Zhu Xi, quoted by Baba, describing the forces of *hun* and *po* in relation to the activity of *zhijue*:

> *Yin* presides over storage and reception and *yang* presides over movements and applications (*yunyong* 運用). In general, the ability to memorize is all due to what *po* stores and receives, but the movements and applications manifested outward are *hun*. These two thing-events are fundamentally inseparable from each other. What enables memorization is *po*, but what manifests outward must be *hun*. That which enables *zhijue* is *po*, but that which manifests *zhijue* outward is *hun*. Each of them belongs respectively to *yin* and *yang*, but within these *yin* and *yang* there are further *yins* and *yangs* [陰主藏受，陽主運用。凡能記憶，皆魄之所藏受也，至於運用發出來是魂。這兩箇物事本不相離。他能記憶底是魄，然發出來底便是魂；能知覺底是魄，然知覺發出來底又是魂。雖各自分屬陰陽，然陰陽中又各自有陰陽也]. (qtd. in Baba 2017: 310; bracketed material is our own, from the original at Zhu Xi 2011b: passage 87)

Here we see that "perception" is dependent upon memorization, which is described as a *yin*-process responsible for the heart-mind's ability to receive and retain what it learns. But via its *yang* aspect, "perception" also "manifests outward" (*fachulai* 發出來). What does this mean?

We understand Zhu's Xi's notion of "outward manifestation" in light of his commentary on the meaning of "extending knowledge" (*zhizhi* 致知) in the *Daxue* (大學), where he says thoughts or intentions (*yi* 意) are what the mind "emits" or sends forth (*fa* 發) (Zhu Xi 2011a),[5] as well as with his comments elsewhere that the extension of knowledge means to "enter into things" (see Adler 2004: 133). Both ideas underscore the sense in which the psychical energies of human thoughts and emotions can, at times, extend beyond the borders of the body. In fact, Zhu observes that "human *qi* and the *qi* of the cosmos are constantly interacting" (qtd. in Adler 2004: 125), which underscores the irreducibly relational constitution of the knowing mind.

That said, we are not always in tune with these energetic interactions or capable of managing them efficaciously. This is why, as Adler says, in Zhu Xi's thought "there is a moral imperative for learning, and the process of learning is a psycho-spiritual transformation that refines and clarifies one's *qi*" (2004: 132). This process of refining and clarifying *qi* helps to develop the "epistemological potential" of the sage that Adler discussed earlier. As he goes on to explain: "Only sages have minds that can penetrate and comprehend the totality of the natural/moral order. This ability also gives them 'talents,' such as precognition, that make them appear 'like spirits' to ordinary people" (2004: 141). In particular, as the *qi* of the sage's mind becomes increasingly refined, sensitive, and agile, the sage enters into extraordinary relations with the surrounding environment: "When the mind's capacity for psycho-physical intercourse with things . . . is developed to the highest degree, it is called 'spiritual' (*shen*), or 'spiritual clarity' (*shenming*)" (2004: 134).

One key feature of a general *qi*-based philosophy that enables such "spiritual clarity" is the recursive behavior of *qi*, or its ability to interact with itself in its different phases to produce increasingly complex manifestations. For example, as types of mind-*qi*, the forces of *hun* and *po* can be described as mental processes or aspects of human capacities, but they can also be described as distinct energies with their own dynamic agency. In fact, several Daoist traditions recognize no less than three *hun* and seven *po*, which come to "infuse" in the human fetus at the third and fourth months of gestation, respectively (Miller 2017: 25). Moreover, widespread Chinese beliefs regarding the afterlife attribute various species of ghosts and spirits to the continued existence of these different *hun* and *po* after bodily death. So when Baba emphasizes *zhijue* as a process of manifestation enabled by *hun* and *po*, this does not simply mean that a single human agent imposes its will on the external world; rather, a lively collection of animating forces can emanate from the subject to varying degrees and according to varying circumstances, sometimes under the influence of the conscious mind and sometimes not.

This is a key point, which returns us to the comment by Ames and Rosemont that we humans "do not live our lives inside our skins." Indeed, as contemporary historian Yung Sik Kim explains, the recursive interactions of *qi* mean that an individual's mental life is not restricted to the confines of her physical body:

> Mind, for Zhu Xi, was really nothing but *qi*, its "essential and refreshing" (*jingshuang* 精爽) or "numinous" (*ling* 靈) portion, to be more specific. Thus, *qi* was endowed with qualities of mind, and could interact with the mind. The mind-*qi* interaction was not restricted to man's *qi* and his own mind, but was extended to the *qi* of the outside world and to the minds of others. (2015: 129)

As stated earlier, the fluid energies of mind-*qi* are not categorically different from the congealed energies that constitute physical matter, meaning that mental forces can indeed become palpable externally or even commingle with the energies of other minds. All modes of *qi* are relational to the core and together co-constitute the selves and worlds of our immediate experience.

Because the energies involved in *zhijue* include the two aspects of inner retention and outward emission, Baba chooses to translate the term not as "perception" but as "realization," which better captures a sense of intellectual insight as well as constructive manifestation and practice. As he says, "*Zhijue*, therefore, is not a passive seeing, as it were, of a predetermined reality, but a participatory determination of the world through cultivated appreciations and realizations" (2017: 311). Realization is, in short, the process of manifesting reality. Ultimately, this power of manifestation is the "epistemological potential" of the sage as a "relational knower," whose irreducibly relational and interactional mode of being is the very mark of her influence on the world around her.

This close look at the *qi*-based worldview has helped to reveal the concrete implications of Ames's and Rosemont's claim that persons are "resolutely transactional and collaborative." The *qi*-based philosophies of China ask us to take seriously the possibility that our private thoughts and feelings are not safely contained within our skins; that our inner lives manifest outwardly, as well; and that these outward-bound forces may easily defy our control so long as we lack training. But, with practice and commitment, as both the Ruist and Daoist traditions confirm, we can indeed learn to progress toward the expanded "epistemological potential" signaled by the figure of the sage.

In the Classroom: Epistemological Potential and Philosophical Practice

What does this expanded conception of "relational knowing" mean for how we practice philosophy as professionals or how we teach world philosophies in the classroom? In many ways, we communicate to students what philosophy "is" through the ways we ask them to "do" philosophy in our classes. As a result, the use of eurocentric methodologies, even while teaching diverse content, can still give the impression that all philosophy is, ultimately, cast from the European or Euro-American model.

Recall how we noted in the previous chapter that an openness to different genres is one prerequisite of working with world philosophies.

There, we observed that our set way of practicing philosophy may make us believe that knowledge has been transmitted in different world philosophies solely through one textual mode. We can now describe an assignment used in one of our own classrooms, while teaching a module on Zhu Xi, as an illustrative example of diversifying methodologies. As indicated earlier, Zhu Xi sees reading, memorizing, and reciting texts as processes of *po*-energies crucial to the development of the kind of "perception" that Baba translates as "realization." In order to best attain this potential, Zhu recommends that we first prep the mind for reading by calming it down: "When the mind isn't settled, it doesn't understand proper order [*li* 理]. Presently, should you want to engage in book learning, you must first settle the mind so that it becomes like still water or a clear mirror [心不定，故見理不得。今且要讀書，須先定其心，使之如止水，如明鏡]" (Zhu Xi 2011b: passage 11).[6] Zhu advises that you do some stretching, maybe some deep breathing, and at one point he recommends that you sit still and hum: "In reading, students must compose themselves and sit up straight, look leisurely at the text and hum softly, open their minds and immerse themselves in the words [學者讀書, 須要斂身正坐, 緩視微吟, 虛心涵泳]" (2011b).[7]

When reading this passage with students, one might stress that the key dynamics refer to vibration, resonance, and synchronization. That is, Zhu Xi is asking us to tune in to the text, or to open our minds to the way the text itself resonates. This helps to frame a classroom discussion of *qi* and *qi*-cosmology in concrete terms. Rather than an abstract theory or a rigid system of metaphysical correspondences, Zhu Xi's comments help give students the sense that *qi*-cosmological forces are enacted in concrete practices of self-cultivation—in this case, the act of reading is revealed to be a method for refining and clarifying *qi*. As Zhu Xi says, "The value of a book is in the recitation of it. By reciting it often, we naturally come to understand it [書只貴讀，讀多自然曉]. . . . I don't know how the mind so naturally harmonizes with the *qi*, feels uplifted and energized, and remembers securely what it reads [這箇不知如何，自然心與氣合，舒暢發越，自是記得牢]."[8] In other words, to read a book is to palpably imprint on the mind, and to memorize and recite that book, as a method of *qi*-cultivation, is to sustain those effects on the mind. Because the knowing mind is relational to its core, it is capable of this transformative interchange with texts. Earlier we considered the *hun*-energy of outward manifestation as a mark of the sage's influence on others; here we see that the *po*-energy of reception and retention speaks to the equally radical openness of the relational knower to the influence of ideas, minds, and environments around her.

For Zhu Xi, this is the power of learning, the transformative power of philosophy. The larger goal might be to transform one's own mind into the mind of a sage, but mostly Zhu seems happy with students who can transform themselves into literate, well-cultivated, and, most of all, humane members of society. In line with the discussion of manuscript-based cultures in Chapter 2, classics and the commentaries on them compose a repository of living documents whose transmission is central to the practice of Chinese philosophy. So, despite initial resistance from students, we have found it to be effective to have them memorize a text when teaching Song-dynasty Ruist philosophers like Zhu Xi. Memorization marks a concrete and sustained engagement with the relational mode of knowing found in Ruist thought. Moreover, it is a scholarly methodology indigenous to Ruist tradition, not a European or Euro-American methodology imposed upon the Ruist content.

In the particular classroom assignment described here, students are asked to memorize the opening passages of the Great Learning (*Daxue* 大學), which is a little under 300 words in English. They take it one line at a time, memorizing it cumulatively over the course of the whole semester. About every other week, they have a quiz where they write out what they have learned so far. Sometimes they recite it out loud together, and sometimes they practice "quiet sitting" (*jingzuo* 静坐), a Ruist meditative technique, before reviewing it. Later, they read commentaries on the *Daxue* by Zhu Xi and the later Ming-dynasty philosopher Wang Yangming (1472–1529), and they conclude this semester-long study of the *Daxue* by composing their own commentaries on the text.

Here, the philosophical methodologies used with students involve memorization and recitation as a method of philosophical study; also, certain contemplative practices (quiet sitting) meant to prepare the mind to read; and, finally, commentarial writing as a form a philosophical expression (a preeminently relational mode of philosophical engagement, we might add). The goal here is to have students "do" philosophy with the tools of the philosophical tradition being covered, so as not to simply feed Ruist content into eurocentric paradigms.

And what do the Ruist methods tell students about what philosophy "is"? Many professional philosophers today might say that the core of philosophy is about critical thinking, or rational argumentation, or, even, the perennial search for truth. All three are related to an understanding of philosophy that is, ultimately, static and teleological. It is static in the sense that it involves the analytical decomposition of arguments and assertions—a process that is not open-ended but has a terminal point. It is teleological, then, for that same reason, that is, that one progresses toward a fixed goal, namely, a judgment of truth or validity.

In contrast, the Chinese tradition gives us is a picture of philosophy that is dynamic, creative, and open-ended. It is dynamic in the sense that we mean the active conditioning of the mind to prime it for effective reading and support its continual learning process. Here, critical thinking is not absent, but it is a baseline minimum needed to avoid rudimentary errors in reasoning. Beyond this baseline, philosophy is about conditioning and transforming the mind through scholarly discipline. For that same reason, it is open-ended. The goal of philosophical learning—that is, being a well-cultivated person, or even a sage—is itself framed in terms of a heightened state of flexibility or as a capacity for appropriate responsiveness in unfamiliar situations. Although we strongly support the pedagogical innovations prompted by a relational mode of knowing, we submit that colleagues who have not yet engaged with such work may take this way of doing philosophy to be a flagrant breach of disciplinary norms.

Conclusion: Moving Forward

Our discussion about relational knowing set in by exploring the claim that knowing is a social affair. From this, we went on to explore the concrete extent to which this social self is "transactional and collaborative" to its core, with reference in particular to Chinese *qi*-based models of the heart-mind. But we would be remiss if we did not admit that the "epistemological potential" of the sage, whose cultivated mental energies exert an efficacious pull on the world around her and on the minds of others, must sound simply like esoteric, otherworldly "magic" to philosophers steeped in contemporary eurocentric academic norms. Ames and Rosemont claim that the relational model of personhood "is grounded in and is responsible to our empirical experience" (2016: 12). However, deeply entrenched assumptions within eurocentric thought about the divide between the mental and the material, spiritual and physical, sentient and insentient, and so forth may prevent contemporary philosophers from even entertaining the plausibility of the *qi*-based understanding of lived experience.

All this is to say that erstwhile practices of knowledge making have been continued within academic philosophy at large. Not only do we tend to operate with the standard understanding of philosophical knowledge makers, we also tend to continue extant narratives spun by these knowledge makers about other philosophical traditions. Our discussion, however, revealed that relational knowing may be a powerful tool to disrupt these extant practices. If we should continue to think of knowledge practices as "those collective, routine socio-material ways of carrying on that enable people to say 'we know' with at least some degree of certainty" (Verran 2013: 155), we may have to reconsider how we position European and Euro-American philosophy in the academy. We may, for instance, need to interrogate typical depictions of the world's "wisdom traditions" according to which these relics of the past have no relevance for the pursuits of academic philosophy today. In fact, like Ruism and the epistemological potential it promises, they might just contain (rich) conceptual sources to understand our place in the world.

To sum up: in placing relational knowing front and center, this chapter has followed recent scholarship that attempts to overcome methodological weaknesses in the study of world-philosophical traditions. Relational knowing is a tool, which has been developed to overcome the truncation between a knowing philosophical self, and the world in which he moves (the male pronoun is intended here). This tool takes the social aspect of philosophizing seriously.

In the history of European thought, its dominant philosophical narratives came to suggest that only philosophical tools developed by its own traditions could enable one to track relevant philosophical activity worldwide across time and space. In an attempt at resisting this dominance, some postcolonial comparative philosophers painstakingly drew out apparent philosophical similarities between the positions forwarded in the dominant renditions and their counterparts from world-philosophical traditions. Arguably, this move was necessitated by systemic factors. However, this line of scholarship tended to draw on non-eurocentric scholarship only to fill up perceived gaps, or what Starblanket and Stark call "a *vacancy* or *bankruptcy*" in standard scholarship (2018: 181). Hereby, the power binary between eurocentric philosophy and its world-philosophical counterparts was reproduced and maintained. The radical otherness of the positions studied was largely obliterated; the world of conventional comparative philosophy began to bear an uncanny resemblance to the world of academic philosophy at large. In hindsight we can today see, and rectify, this standard comparative approach.

Today, the rich scholarship referenced even in the pages so far gives us reason, and courage, to leave this self-centered frame of reference behind and to explore the plurality of world philosophies through relational knowing. It invites us to engage in epistemic disconcertment, which can unsettle us and provoke us to rethink our multiple ways of being in the world. This scholarship drives home the point that when a theory does not allow for "a social and political critique of the conditions of its own enunciation," it may tend to "overstate its emancipatory potential, and even mask a universalizing—even if dialogical disposition" (Rivera 2019: 108).

Discussion Questions

- In your own words, distinguish between positions of relativism, absolutism, and pluralism. How would you respond to a person who claims that this chapter's call for "pluralizing methodologies" amounts to simple relativism?
- What does the standard view mean when it claims that the philosophical self always generates culturally invariant results? Find some examples to substantiate your view.
- Can you come up with reasons as to why the standard view of philosophy chooses to bracket the knowing-how dimension?
- Why should the manner in which we know in our daily lives have any significance for the way we do professional philosophy?
- Can you make sense of the claim that some knowers experience themselves as multiplicitous selves from your own perspective?

4

Knowledge Claims and Locality

The Grand Narrative of Universal Knowledge

Chapter 3 has given us a first glimpse of how one could set upon the path of knowing world philosophies relationally. If followed, this path would affect the manner in which we study world philosophies. Equally, it would impact upon some standard notions of conceiving philosophical practice. Take, for example, the view that true philosophy remains a decontextualized, culturally invariant mode of inquiry, meaning that its tools remain detached from their place of origin (namely Europe and North America) and that these tools are applicable to complex phenomena of philosophical significance across the globe. To use Emmanuel Chukwudi Eze's analogy, this standard view operates with the notion of academic philosophy as if it were a "chemical catalyst [which remains] unchanged by the very things whose analysis makes its own activity possible" (2001: 206).

As Eze notes, this view rests on an "ultra-faith" that is not corroborated through practice (2010: 207). A closer study of this practice would reveal how philosophical beliefs, suppositions, and theories were formed and influenced by specific sociopolitical factors at particular moments in time. The belief in an ahistorical, transcendental, and universal mode of philosophical operation is itself a particular development specific to a sociopolitical context.

The point that the current self-positioning of academic philosophy may be directly related to relatively recent historical developments can be adumbrated by drawing on parts of Marshall G. S. Hodgson's (1922–1968) work. By 1800, Western Europe, which hitherto had been a "frontier region" in "interregional interchange," began dominating other regions (Hodgson 1993: 21, 27). It centered itself in the world, be it in spatial or temporal representations, as contemporary world maps and an evolutionist view of global history reveal. In both cases, "our own [European] cultural ancestors hold most of the attention" (Hodgson 1993: 6). One result of this self-positioning was that Western Europe's practices of scientific or artistic borrowing became invisible. To put it differently: this world region extracted itself from the process of interregional exchange with the help of a narrative that was conveniently "lifted out of its context and elevated into a self-creating entity unto itself" as Charles Mills states (2017: 61).

Hodgson notes one curious feature of this self-centering: Western Europe's self-affirmation as being a unique civilization in human history is widely accepted across the globe today. Furthermore, historical and geographical terms emanating from this self-positioning are taken as being "indiscriminately scientific" by people located outside Western Europe (Hodgson 1993: 7). In consequence, Western Europe's narrative of itself, and its place in the world, have become relatively universal background presumptions in academic inquiry. Hodgson urges us not to accept this standard view: "Modernity is simply 'Western' neither in its origins, nor in its impact as a world event, nor even as an expression of cultural continuity; above all, not in the nature of the cultural problems it raises for us all" (1993: 28). More recently Shahzad Bashir, sharing Hodgson's observations, has used the term "spatiotemporal Eurocentrism" to point out the ubiquitous nature of the centering of Western European thought persistent in academia today (2017: 22).

Hodgson's account of world history cannot be thoroughly analyzed within the scope of our volume. The approach itself can be extended in the context of our inquiry though. For one, it urges us to be more skeptical about the standard view that philosophical theory is—and can only be—produced in certain parts of the world, namely Europe and North America. It seems more plausible to assume that theories arise, and have arisen, in different parts of the globe. Furthermore, theories move with their proponents, travel with them in space and time, and change as a result of these encounters. Clearly, the narrative that the European and Euro-American philosophical tradition is culturally superior should arouse suspicion. But the specific geopolitical factors at particular periods in time, which gave rise to this contingent historic curiosity, merit closer analysis.

In this regard, Hodgson's approach supplements some insights of our last chapter from a world-historical perspective. Not only do his thoughts urge us to become more skeptical of grand narratives and universalizing theories, but they also push us to critically engage with the eurocentric categories we have inherited in the process of our intellectual socialization, regardless of our particular locations across the globe. As Bashir states: "To be operational as an epistemological structuring principle, Eurocentrism does not require its upholders to identify as Europeans" (2017: 23). Only when we acknowledge the hold of eurocentrism on our own intellectual categories, can we engage with its historical contingency and slowly begin to work out other ways of understanding philosophical inquiry into selves, worlds, and ways of knowing. But there is more.

We can use Hodgson's appeal to decenter the conventional narrative prevalent in the academy to further our own thoughts about a philosophical inquiry into world philosophies. For example, one could argue that our philosophical inquiry should not be reined in by the worry that a focus on local practices could end up in relativism. Why, for example, be led by the standard claim that only the eurocentric philosophical tradition can generate universal knowledge? Why take the belief for granted that every step away from this tradition would necessarily lead us into relativism? Unless, we are willing to concede that our search for universal knowledge is tied up with other motivations like "academic comfort" or "the complacent enjoyment of narrow departmental power" (Eze 2010: 209), we, as philosophers, may have to engage historical evidence about such claims. And from what we know today, we can conclude that the purported universal reach of European reason is nothing but a circumstantial claim.

Another possible upshot of this line of thought would be that "Europe" may itself be more plural than taken at first glance. It may be a conglomerate "of plural entities with mixed histories of genesis" (Mayar and Guevara Gonzalez 2017: 4). The reference to a single, coherent, and unified whole could itself reflect complex processes of "benchmarking" (2017: 4) through which different ways of self-positioning that took place within this cultural space were consolidated into one. We may need to study the plurality of local practices in Europe then. Hereby, we may also need to be mindful of the creative cross-pollination that took place on the ground there and later in North America. Within the context of world philosophies, we may, as a corollary, need to consider the possibility that we are dealing with plural eurocentrisms, given that eurocentrism may have been experienced differently in specific locales.

Arguably, human history has known other forms of group domination, too, and the binary between the dominators and the dominated is rarely clear-cut. And yet, the philosophical canon worldwide continues to bear an undeniably eurocentric stamp. So, how would relational knowing change what we know of world philosophies? Would this way of knowing prompt us in any way to reflect on the methodological choices we make when we study world philosophies? The short answer is that the relational knower will always seek to contextualize her understanding of any given philosophical study, whether this involves historical context, sociopolitical context, cultural context, or other. This methodological approach is somewhat at odds with contemporary analytic methodologies, which often utilize intentionally decontextualized thought experiments and the purposefully abstract language of symbolic proofs. These tools are not discarded by the relational knower but are, in fact, understood to be useful within certain philosophical contexts, which are themselves best appreciated in light of their historical and cultural development—in the case of analytic philosophy, the reaction of British scholars to then-dominant European idealism in the early twentieth century. Indeed, when we understand the radical intervention that British analytic philosophy once posed to the European mainstream, we can better appreciate its continued potential for progressive thought today.

Above all, the relational knower will seek to contextualize even the universal claims of philosophy. This is not to deny universalizing aims or resort to relativism but rather to underscore the context in which a given universal claim makes its most potent intervention in philosophical thought, is best positioned to challenge unexamined assumptions, or can most effectively transform our understanding of ourselves and our worlds. Let us study the debate on personhood in African philosophy to illustrate this point.

Methodological Holism and the Becoming of a Person

On the basis of extant linguistic conventions, one could make a case for segregating an understanding of a human being from that of a person. As Ifeanyi Menkiti (1984: 171) in his essay "Person and Community in Traditional African Thought" argues, "in the African view it is the community which defines the person as a person, not some isolated static quality of rationality, will or memory" (1984: 172). Accordingly, this notion of personhood is not a universal, *a priori* attribution to all human beings. Rather, whether a human being is a person or not depends on whether the behavior of this being conforms to certain role-based norms of responsibility-taking. Personhood is constituted by fulfilling these norms. Thus, gradations of personhood depend on concrete circumstances. Even within one's own lifetime, one and the same human being can reach, and move away from, different levels of personhood. Personhood, if you will, is not a conferred status, but an achievement of "social self-hood": "[P]ersonhood is something at which individuals could fail, at which they could be competent or ineffective, better or worse" (1984: 173). African grief patterns at funerals of infants, Menkiti argues, are a case in point. Ritualized grief for the deceased of this age-group is relatively absent; it increases with the age of the deceased, which, as Menkiti claims, correlates with the development of personhood.

Kwame Gyekye sharply contests this view in his "Person and Community in Akan Thought" (2010). Minimalized grief patterns for infants, Gyekye reasons, could have to do with ameliorating the grief of surviving relatives, and the larger existential issues arising from this loss. Moreover, he claims, Menkiti misinterprets the larger point: "Personhood may reach its full realization in a community, but it is not achieved or yet to be realized as one goes along in society" (2010: 109). Rather, personhood reflects society's evaluation of, and respect for, the exercise of an individual's moral agency. Expressions like *oye onipa paa* ("somebody is a real human being"), *onipa hun* ("useless person"), or *onnye 'nipa* ("wicked or bad person") illustrate these different evaluations. Importantly though, the individual's moral agency continues to be respected in every single one of them. Gyekye interprets these evaluations as attributions of social status, which do not detract from the inherent personhood of a human being (2010: 112). For Gyekye, Akan linguistic conventions attribute respect to all human beings on virtue of their possession of the "divine spark called soul (*okra)*" (2010: 115).

Arguably, the conventional methodology in comparative philosophy would take an exchange such as this as typifying the discourse on African personhood, after which the next step would be to juxtapose it against its "western" counterpart. Our relational knower will not halt here though. Rather than immediately turn the comparison into one about "the West" and "the other," she will continue to engage with the subject in context to appreciate the nuanced and complex diversity within African thought. Such a process points her to broader, currently ongoing methodological discussions, which would be overlooked by too quickly invoking the methodologies of Euro-American traditions. Let us follow the relational knower's trail here to see what else she finds.

Bernard Matolino (2011), for example, also critiques Menkiti's personhood interpretation. To understand his critique, let us turn once again to Menkiti—this time to his essay "On the Normative Conception of a Person" (2005). Here, Menkiti, in Matolino's reading, interprets African personhood as an "ontological progression" in the journey from being a baby to becoming a spiritual ancestor. In this journey, the former, a gender-neutral "it" without individuality, matures into a person and then turns into another gender-neutral "it"—an ancestor—whose human personhood recedes slowly. This journey from one "it" to another "it" does not bridge the present with the future. It joins the present with the past. The "more of a past one has, the more standing as a person one also has." The qualities one gathers through lived experience are "not only qualitatively superior to, but also ontologically different" from the ones one possessed at the beginning of this journey (2005: 325). Against this background, personhood is not a blanket attribution of moral status to every human body. Rather, it is a "notion of moral arrival," a status achieved during one's life through complex social processes of norm internalization and individual transformation. After dying though, the "nameless dead remain *its*, and cannot be designated as something else" (2005: 328; emphasis in original).

Matolino contests Menkiti's postulation of this "matter of cultural fact" (2005: 330) in Africa. In paraphrasing the former's analysis, let it be noted that two strands are intertwined here: conceptual analysis and an evaluation of the description's accuracy. In short: Matolino critically examines the conceptual framework of Menkiti's position on personhood and considers whether this position can be said to be an adequate description of African personhood. Let us begin with the first prong.

For Matolino, when "it" is used in English as a referential word, it would be wrong to interpret this use as giving us more information about the moral and ontological status of the entity it refers to. In the context of personhood, the term "it," can under certain circumstances be used for males and females too. Furthermore, Menkiti's use of "it" for depersonalized existence at the beginning and end of life occludes the difference in the status attributed to a baby and an ancestor. While the former has yet to become a person, the latter was already one and will through its death now lose personhood gradually. So, the ancestor and the baby cannot be thought of as being the same it. In short: Menkiti, in Matolino's opinion, wrongly suggests that there is no ontological progression between life and death, when in fact there is. This is not all. Menkiti's suggestion of an ontological progression during the different stages of life mistakes this progression for an epistemological progression. Children and elders are separated not through their ontological differences but through the "epistemological superiority" of the latter, which in turn will affect their respective performance of roles (Matolino 2011: 35).

This analysis suffices to briefly deal with the second prong: Matolino holds that Menkiti's understanding of an "it" cannot be corroborated by its use in several African languages, including Menkiti's native Igbo (2011: 28). Even the claim that the ancestors' form of existence changes, when future generations render their ancestors nameless, cannot be sustained: "This particular reference to the departed as having no personhood status is a gross violation of the African understanding of the status of the departed" (2011: 31). Matolino's concern in this regard seems to be that Menkiti's view inaccurately suggests that ancestors lose their personhood. In fact, the opposite is true. Becoming an ancestor is closely linked up with becoming a person. "If one fails at personhood one is not likely to succeed at becoming an ancestor" (2011: 31). Those who have led morally upright lives begin a new existence of collective immortality. They "will never go out of that existence" (2011: 31).

In a recent publication, Polycarp Ikuenobe lays out his reasons for holding that Matolino may just have overshot the ball. Ikuenobe's intervention to defend Menkiti seeks to correct both the strands of Matolino's reading mentioned earlier. Neither does Menkiti claim that his account is the only possible way to understand authentic and essential African personhood, nor can Matolino's reading do justice to the larger point Menkiti seeks to make. Ikuenobe concludes that Menkiti's view has "a heuristic value in theorising about the social, political and moral aspects of African cultures" (2017: 566). One key reason is the methodology it adopts.

Ikuenobe directs our attention to the "*methodological holism*" developed in Menkiti's account (2017: 554). Unlike conventional renditions that draw on methodological individualism, this holism does not segregate persons from their embeddedness in communities. It seeks to understand a community as a whole unit. Through this methodological choice, it is able to grasp that "reality [in the African context] is a composite and unity of supernatural and natural elements, energy, and forces that have harmonious interactions" (2017: 555). The meaning of being an individual and/or a community cannot be crystallized in abstraction; it should be understood against the backdrop of this specific understanding of reality.

Accordingly, personhood in Menkiti's account is to be taken as a "thick concept" in which the descriptive and the normative are intermeshed. Contra Matolino, this holistic perspective does not allow for any easy answer on an ontological progression through the different stages of one's life. In fact, Menkiti's holistic lens allows us to better understand the intermeshing between a minimal and a maximal definition of a person in the African context. The former "descriptive metaphysical aspect of personhood is a material condition for the [latter] normative aspect. In order to be called a 'real' or 'true' person who achieves moral personhood, one must satisfy the normative moral criteria. In order to satisfy the normative moral criteria, one must have the descriptive metaphysical or psychological features or capacities such as free will" (2017: 556). To simply separate the ontological element of personhood from other related elements would be to miss out on how the ontological serves as a mere material base for the development of normative personhood. We become persons in and through communities, which for their part connect us to other natural and supernatural entities. Becoming a person in this context entails developing the potentiality and honing the capacities afforded by this community.

Ikuenobe's analysis is salient inasmuch as it invites us to reflect more carefully on the methodological choices we make. To adequately understand the intricacies of personhood in African cultures, we may have to rethink our extant conceptual frameworks. We may have to fine-tune them if we wish to obtain a better grip on the context at hand. In our immediate context, methodological individualism may simply not be the appropriate lens, even if it is taken to be such by default. Here, methodological holism may be more appropriate.

Using the holistic lens not only brings to light different aspects of personhood, as it is understood in some African cultures, but it can also correct extant understandings of the same. As one such interpretation will have it, a normative understanding of an African community cannot make place for individual rights given that it does not operate with personhood as a universal attribute. But as we saw, Menkiti's distinction between a minimal and maximal understanding of personhood makes clear that the issue at hand is not whether biological and metaphysical entities we commonly call human beings are in fact so. Rather, this distinction highlights the work communities must accomplish, should their members, who are human beings, be able to become persons.

Menkiti is, to be sure, making a universal claim about personhood. But only by understanding this claim in context, with all the complexities of Indigenous African philosophy and neocolonial African political realities, can the relational knower begin to appreciate the extent to which this universal claim might speak to her, personally, in the present. In other words, one might assume that the best procedure for transformative comparative engagement is to build bridges between African and European or Euro-American traditions. But in fact it is by diving deeper and deeper into the African context that frames the personhood debates that we cease to exoticize African thought as the "other" of "western" thought or reduce it immediately to eurocentric paradigms; and only in this way do we position our own understanding of "personhood" so as to be open to transformation by African models.

Overall, Menkiti's position should be understood less as a concrete metaphysical claim about what African personhood is, but more as a call for a community to involve its members in its communal vision of what it means to be a normative entity. To do so appropriately, it would have to provide at least some goods to the individual so that the latter can work to contribute to this vision. But Ikuenobe's correction may not be the last word on personhood in African cultures either—the more we explore, the more complex the context grows.

Being-with-Others and Gendered Being

Another line of critique against accounts endorsing "beingness-with-others" (Menkiti) in the African context is launched by those who object to "gender-blind essentialism" of the said accounts (Oyowe and Yurkivska 2014: 87). According to Oritsegbubemi A. Oyowe and Olga Yurkivska, for example, standard accounts of African personhood fail to adequately consider that the African understanding of being a person is gendered. "[T]o be a person, by definition, is to be related, i.e.

to be placed within a complex web of communal social relationships and the latter are gendered" (2014: 93). So, how can a reappropriation of Indigenous conceptual resources liberate "both women and men from severely constricting gender scripts" (du Toit and Coetzee 2017: 335)? One answer can be found within the discussion on personhood in African cultures itself.

Oyèrónkẹ́ Oyěwùmí, for example, argues that precolonial Yorùbá society was not organized along the lines of sex or gender. Instead of using the body as a marker, precolonial Yorùbá society organized its members on the basis of the roles the latter played in the society. As a result, the understanding of being a person was fleshed out depending upon the roles one inhabited. The understanding of sexuate bodies, which came in with coloniality, not only affected the manner in which society was organized after colonialism. It has affected the translation of crucial terms too. *Obinrin* and *Okunrin*, which are translated today as female/woman and male/man respectively, have less to do with sexuated bodies; rather, *rin* points to the common humanity dwelling in these bodies. Accordingly, both sex and gender are relatively new developments in Yorùbá communities, which in history have operated with notions of gender fluidity.

Arguably, this possible response may not wholly address the concerns of scholars like Oyowe and Yurkivska. They seem to be pointing out that important conceptual work—like that of Oyěwùmí—should not be taken as the ultimate fix for today's gender-related issues. Foregrounding notions of role-based morality may indeed be helpful in correcting the individualistic lives we moderns live. However, these notions may have to be supplemented by others that are geared to address issues pertaining to our daily lives, like for example property and marriage law. However, to read Oyěwùmí's work in this light would be to miss her larger point on decolonizing the mind and body.

Oyěwùmí pushes back against "genderism" and against the "idea that male dominance in human affairs is universal and timeless" (2011: 31). In adopting a blanket genderist lens, she says, one may be doing disservice to practices available on the ground. This lens may lead one to believe that throughout human history, social distinctions have been understood in the same way across time and space, or that Indigenous resources are completely blind to today's gender-related concerns. However, there is no hard-and-fast rule that all societies must be "somatocentric" in her view (1999: 183). "The preoccupation with body parts as a means of grounding social distinctions is by no means universal and, therefore, should not be assumed of other cultures, rather, it should be explored" (1999: 184).

Oyěwùmí uses her work on Yorùbá to show that there have indeed been other ways of conceiving human relations, which do not necessarily operate with a body-mind dichotomy. These alternative ways do not necessarily posit certain predetermined attributions of the human body as the point zero in every deliberation about human existence. They develop social categories, which cannot necessarily be traced back to the notion of an unchanging human body. It would be simplistic to claim that a reappropriation of these notions is atavistic. Rather, an adequate reappropriation of Indigenous sources may open up other ways in imagining "multiple ways of being in the same human body in one world" (1999: 188). So, again, we underscore the idea that an ever-deepening exploration of philosophical context—that is, the practice of relational knowing—is the best strategy for fully appreciating the contemporaneous voice of a given tradition, whose claims to universality might indeed reach out to include us in its scope. It is precisely this level of context that books in the *Bloomsbury Introductions to World Philosophies* seek to provide.

In the Classroom: Universality and Locality in Philosophical Practice

Standard ways of mapping world-philosophical traditions through the cross-cultural or comparative lens have tended to organize philosophical content along geographical lines. Some of these labels are wedded to nation-states and others to whole continents. Terms like "Indian philosophy," "Chinese philosophy," "Japanese philosophy," and so on follow the former pattern, while "African philosophy," "Latin American philosophy," and "Asian philosophy" follow the latter. Other standard approaches have used seemingly ethnic designations or linguistic ones. In many cases, there is substantial overlap. For example, when we speak of "Japanese philosophy," do we mean the philosophy practiced by citizens of the nation-state of Japan, the philosophy practiced by the "ethnic" Japanese, or the philosophy conducted in the Japanese language?

At a first glance, one notable exception to these various standard orderings is the field designated "Islamic philosophy." As the name seems to indicate, this is a field that is independent of a particular geographical region or that speaks to an intellectual history that spans multiple regions. However, as Bashir analyzes, this is not wholly true. Scholarly Islam, says Bashir, posits a "timeless Middle Eastern culture" as its center and regards other perspectives, which have been produced away from this center, as "being forever derivative on one hand and encumbered with accretions from 'other' cultures on the other" (Bashir 2014: 529).[1] Other relatively recent additions to cross-cultural philosophy, such as "Jewish philosophy" and "Indigenous philosophy," similarly challenge the conventional geographical lens through which our worlds of philosophy are structured. However, it is too early to tell how these various emerging fields relate to the usual geographic and linguistic schema of cross-cultural and comparative philosophy (and we will have more to say about our approach to these categories, as series editors, in our final chapter).

In all cases—whether we adhere to a geographical organization, or a linguistic one, or we speak of transregional intellectual lineages—the standard way of presenting cross-cultural philosophical material suggests that separable units (the "traditions") can indeed boast of "authentic" and "essential" ways of understanding the world.

In this rendition, only the philosophical traditions of Europe and North America remain unmarked—they appear, in general, without geographical tags (such as "American philosophy"), ethnic designations ("white philosophy"), or linguistic categories ("English philosophy"). This conflation of "Euro-American philosophy" with "just philosophy" reflects a condition well captured by what Bret Davis calls not simply "philosophical Eurocentrism" but "philosophical Euromonopolism" (2020: 18).

With regards to Japanese material in particular, Davis says that the question "What is Japanese philosophy?" involves at least three issues: (1) ontological assumptions behind our inquiry into the "whatness" of a given tradition, (2) the perpetually debated definition of "philosophy" in general, and (3) the question, as raised earlier, about the meaning of the descriptor "Japanese" in this context (2020: 1). The second issue speaks to the history of the translation of the terms "philosophy" and "religion" into Japanese in the Meiji period, as discussed in Chapter 2. As such, the meaning of "Japanese philosophy," whatever this turns out to be, already involves a cross-cultural exchange. This is as true of the traditions of Buddhist and Ruist scholarship in Japan as it is of contemporary academic philosophy. Davis's larger point is that no apparently cohesive "tradition" is entirely insular, unalloyed, or unequivocal; rather, all strands of philosophical inquiry bear the marks of diverse influences, including so-called Greek philosophy, which, as he says, "was not born in Athens but rather in the intensely cross-cultural setting of the Greek colonies in Asia Minor" (2020: 29).

The third issue—that is, the meaning of the designation "Japanese" in this context—further highlights problematic assumptions regarding cultural purity and cultural relativism that often attend the mapping of world-philosophical traditions. As Davis says, through his engagement with the influential work of Robert Bernasconi, there is an apparent tension between the notion that true philosophy is fundamentally about universal claims and the notion that philosophy is culturally Greek in origin (2020: 36–7). Davis wants to avoid the apparent relativism of reducing all philosophy to area studies (Japanese philosophy, Greek philosophy, and so forth[2]) while at the same time avoiding the cultural chauvinism of claiming that some cultures and not others had special access to universal reason. He proposes:

> Thus, it could be said that each act of philosophizing enacts *a particular approach to universality*, and we have no access to universality that bypasses these particular approaches. . . . For example, if I say that humans are mortal, I am not just saying that humans who speak my language and who belong to my culture and tradition are mortal. I am attempting to state a universal truth. And, yet, the sense and significance of "mortality," not to mention specific views of how to live in the face of our universal condition of mortality, will always be colored by the particularities of our languages, cultures, and traditions. This is not to say that we are locked into the horizons of these particularities, but we always begin to philosophize from somewhere. (2020: 53–4)

With this established, Davis proposes a distinction between "Japanese philosophy" and "philosophy in Japan," where the former means "*any rigorous reflection on fundamental questions that draws sufficiently and significantly on the intellectual, linguistic, cultural, religious, literary, and artistic sources of the Japanese tradition*" (2020: 60; emphasis in original). This definition includes the caveat that these very linguistic, cultural, and artistic sources are themselves the products of rich intellectual cross-cultural exchange, and it allows for the possibility that Japanese philosophy is done both inside and outside the borders of today's nation-state by philosophers who may or may not be themselves of Japanese ancestry (for a similar point, see Chapter 5).

In this context, it would do well to recall our discussion from Chapter 2 regarding the four-part schema for "religion" that traditionally included Christianity, Islam, Judaism, and a fourth ambiguous category variously described as "heathenism," "paganism," or "idolatry." In that schema, Christianity held a privileged place as the one, true, universal religion, while Judaism and Islam enjoyed less prestige as precursors to Christianity (in the case of Judaism) or offshoots of it (in the case of Islam); but both were included thanks to their membership in a shared biblical heritage and shared monotheistic theology. The final category referred not to this shared heritage, which marked the borders of religion "proper" for European scholars and theologians, but rather to the diverse practices of the Americas, Africa, and Oceania, which were excluded from the category of religion and branded heretical or even possibly demonic.

As Tomoko Masuzawa demonstrates in *The Invention of World Religions*, this latter designation was kept in place, in one form or another, as the category "religion" grew to include more and more members. The emerging discourse on "world religions" in the eighteenth century was marked by a tension: one the one hand, the term could be used to refer simply to the collection of religions around the globe; on the other hand, it could refer specifically to the "world-historical" religions in a quasi-Hegelian sense, which is to say, the religions that somehow transcend mere "tribalism" via some aspiration toward universal truth (Masuzawa 2005: 12–13). This tension remains today: more often than not, the apparent neutrality of the first sense is, upon closer inspection, underwritten by the civilizational hierarchy implied by the second.

Take many of the common textbooks in world religions today as an example. Huston Smith's dated but still highly influential *The World's Religions* contains chapters on Hinduism, Buddhism, Confucianism, Taoism, Islam, Judaism, and Christianity, with a final chapter titled "The Primal Religions." This "mode of religiosity," Huston explains, "continues in Africa, Australia, Southeast Asia, the Pacific Islands, Siberia, and among the Indians of North and South America." (2009: 365).[3] Or, consider a more recent textbook: John Bowker's *World Religions* (2006). It contains core chapters on Hinduism, Buddhism, Jainism, Sikhism, "Chinese and Japanese Religions," Judaism, Christianity, and

Islam (note how some religions are referenced by designated names and others by geographic region). These core chapters are preceded by a chapter titled "Ancient Religions," focusing on the pre-Christian practices of Egypt, the Mediterranean, and Europe; and the book ends with a final chapter on "Native Religions," covering most of the same regions specified by Huston as "primal." For one more example, Christopher Partridge's *Introduction to World Religions* (2018) begins with a chapter on "Religions of Antiquity," which itself begins with a section titled "Religions before History"—a Hegelian designation if ever there was one. The volume then includes a chapter on "Indigenous Religions," covering, again, the regions specified by Huston; and after this, the main chapters proceed in order via Hinduism, Buddhism, Jainism, "Chinese Religions," "Korean and Japanese Religions," Judaism, Christianity, Islam, and Sikhism.

What unites the practices in regions as diverse as the Americas, Oceania, and Africa, such that they should be classified together in a single chapter? As Masuzawa shows, this chapter is a direct descendent of the hierarchical mapping of world civilizations that recognizes some traditions as "world-historical" and others as "perhaps not so great . . . which tend to go by certain generic lower-case names (such as shamanism and animism)" (2005: 3). She clarifies:

> The category in its entirety used to be uniformly called 'primitive religions' in the earlier days, but more recently it has been variously termed "primal," "pre-literate," "tribal." . . . The restless shifting of appellations may be a measure of the discomfort felt by contemporary scholars of religion in their effort not to appear condescending to those peoples who used to be referred to as savages. (2005: 4)

Once upon a time, the practitioners of Buddhism and Ruism would have been included in this same category, along with other "idolators" around the globe. But, under the influence of a quasi-Hegelian ranking of world cultures, some religions in the "paganism" category were eventually elevated to the status of a "world religion" and, as such, now occupy their own chapters in world religions textbooks.[4] So, as this discussion makes clear, the paganism category has not gone away entirely—it has been preserved under some title such as "Primal Religions," "Native Religions," and, most directly relevant to our own concerns here, "Indigenous Religions." We could not possibly miss the fact that the members of the field known as Indigenous philosophy today mirror the regions covered by the terms "primal" and "native" in many world religions textbooks.

And yet Indigenous philosophy also marks out an important and potent area of philosophical intervention. As a site of reclaimed power, the field of Indigenous philosophy forges sociopolitical solidarity across diverse groups of people brought together via the contingent historical conditions of the European colonial period. Thus, when adequately contextualized, the term "Indigenous philosophy" allows us to see how relational knowing forges solidarity, establishes sites for reclaiming power, and as such accomplishes concrete sociopolitical activism. Indeed, Indigenous studies at large has perhaps gone farther than any other field in resisting the hegemony of eurocentric scholarly methodologies in academia. The current efforts to "indigenize the academy" through a re-narration of academic spaces and places (Anderson, Ruiz, Stewart, and Tlostanova 2019) not only speaks to a shared set of sociopolitical concerns, centered on issues of coloniality, imperialism, and, often, environmental and ecological activism. It promises to develop further correctives of influential academic paradigms (see Stewart 2017) as also modes of thought that can better shed light on the Indigenous insight that "things in the world are collapsed within any one thing" (Mika 2017: 2; also Waters 2001).

Against the backdrop of our discussion in this chapter, let us return briefly to our classroom experience. We hope that the following example can illustrate how world philosophies can be taught even in settings that have had hitherto relatively minimal exposure to cross-cultural philosophical work.

Co-conducted with an Indigenous philosopher, the course we reference sought to examine the recent call for epistemic decolonization in philosophy. This decolonization can be understood as "the aim and process of undoing Eurocentrism, the unwarranted centering of Western knowledge, which justified Western imperialism, and now obfuscates its ongoing legacies" (Kim 2019: 40). Three-fourths of course readings dealt with texts considered to be important to critical theory; the rest was dedicated to Indigenous philosophy. After the class had worked through the standard readings, the Indigenous philosopher introduced her own work. The latter focuses on Indigenous concepts of becoming instead of representational knowing, on the assimilatory forces of the academy, and the pressure to present Indigenous philosophy through the standard molds adopted by academic philosophy. Ample time was allotted for students to reflect on whether they in any way experienced the transformative force of philosophy, since the whiteness of philosophy is—at least at the time of writing these pages—the norm in their particular geographical setting, a norm that has yet to be cognized, thematized, and critiqued adequately.

Going by the feedback we received, the presence of the Indigenous philosopher in person served to disrupt students' standard understanding of who a philosopher is, and should be. In addition, the philosopher's work familiarized them with topics that they had not encountered in any of their university courses before. Moreover, a close engagement with this work—especially against the backdrop of standard readings—made them grasp that eurocentric theory cannot adequately capture all, or other ways of being, notwithstanding its contrary claims. As students' feedback indicates, they could through the course better understand some of the motivation driving the call for epistemic decolonization in philosophy.

The teaching example sketched in Chapter 3 illustrated how to "do" philosophy with the tools covered by the tradition studied. It was meant to highlight how the standard interpretation of philosophy comes up short when it deals with other traditions which operate with a wholly different understanding of philosophy. Our example of Indigenous philosophy in this chapter also does not align well with the standard understanding of philosophy. Much like our example from the Chinese tradition, it is dynamic, creative, and open-ended. And yet, we hope that we have been able to show how its inclusion in a standard philosophy class can disrupt conventional ways of practicing philosophy and transform the mind, even while engaging with standard European and Euro-American theory. Indeed, the format of co-teaching is itself a practice of relational knowing that decenters authority, disrupts conventional classroom hierarchies, and concretely enacts a set of skills important to the world-philosophical approach. While the pedagogical innovations prompted by relational knowing may indeed depart from disciplinary norms in radical ways, they can be easily practiced in a variety of different settings.

Conclusion: Moving Forward

Many external pressures and competing commitments have produced the set of terms commonplace in comparative and cross-cultural philosophy today. In Europe and North America, one could say, the geographic, linguistic, and sometimes "ethnic" way of mapping traditions has, arguably, resulted from painstaking attempts at integrating cross-cultural content into extant philosophical curricula. In other words, there is pressure to retain terms that are understandable within the mainstream, and to work within existing curricular structures, so as to reach a larger audience. In other cases, such as when the term "Indigenous philosophy" is used as a self-description to reclaim a site of power, the use itself can be read as a way of resisting colonial categories in academic philosophy.

As our discussion in this chapter indicates, the standard way of presenting cross-cultural material as the default approach needs to be rectified for two reasons: For one, we have reason to critically study the positioning of the European and Euro-American philosophical tradition itself, just as we have attempted to briefly sketch in these pages. If this tradition claims to be "complete in terms of its roots and relevance," this claim must be backed up by evidence (Schutte 2000: 15). And if this self-affirmation is itself, as we have reason to believe, a historical curiosity, then changes to the dominant narrative are possible. For another, a study of local debates indicates that, at least in some contexts, there is a vigorous debate on whether the positions reflect their geographical tags adequately.

Indeed, the power disparity in knowledge production may have led philosophers in the past to offer "exotic expressions" of world-philosophical modes of being as a form of "necessary" but "forced" protest (Matolino: 2018: 337). Negotiating a path between eurocentric academic philosophy and their own embeddedness in cultural traditions, many began "rejecting a world that [they] may [have] just as well recognize[d], but [could] not accept on the grounds that it [was taken to be] insufficiently philosophical (2018: 341).

Today, however, a vocal number of philosophers, some of whom featured in our reflections, work toward changing the hold of eurocentrism on their own philosophical categories, as our exploration into the debate on personhood in African cultures revealed. These scholars endeavor to critically reappropriate Indigenous knowledges, not to map the world but to make sense of the present. Their work subscribes to the development of what authors like Pascah Mungwini term a "polycentric global epistemology" (Mungwini 2013: 9). Critical reappropriation serves as a lynchpin in this movement from the past through the present to the future.

Our engagement with the debate on personhood in African cultures also highlighted that methodological choices may impact our study of world philosophies. With the right dose of critical self-awareness, we may be able to better grasp the local "flavor" of the world-philosophical traditions we study. This is why authors like Mungwini invite scholars working in former colonies "to challenge the rhetoric and seductive lure of universalism," to "decisively identify and pronounce their locus of annunciation" (2017: 7). These authors call for a critical reappropriation of Indigenous categories in the hope that such a reappropriation can lead to an epistemic liberation from eurocentric categories. They seek to correct the "long-distance relationship" between the knowing subject and its truncation from the "here and now" in Africa (Mungwini citing Martín Alcoff 2017: 9). Some of these authors (like Mungwini himself) lean on the literature on epistemic injustice to claim that the process of knowing is deeply affected by the prevalence of conceptual tools that can adequately track experience. As knowers, we must seek to align our conceptual tools with our experiences. However, when philosophical literature in former colonies continues to operate with the notion of a knowing subject, which was not designed to track the specificities of local experiences in Africa in the first place, why should one continue to use this notion as a prime tool in the knowing process?

Discussion Questions

- How is Western Europe's self-affirmation as being a unique civilization reflected in what you learn at the university? Make a list of points in which this self-affirmation becomes visible in your view.
- If multiple eurocentrisms would be a more accurate description of what is experienced on the ground, how would we have to tweak relevant linguistic practices to reflect this experience?
- "Personhood can reach its full realization in a community." What does this sentence mean to you? Does your understanding of a

community encompass only living, human beings? Or would you be open to including other beings in this understanding too?

- Find examples of social categories that relate to an unchanging body. Then, come up with some examples of such categories that can be meaningfully used for the notion of a body in flux.

5

What's in a Name?

Labeling Traditions

Let us continue our journey alongside our relational knower. In this round, let us follow this knower into worlds of philosophy. As mentioned in Chapter 3, a relational knower will attempt to be more sensitive to the possibility that structural prejudices may seep into the act of knowing. For this purpose, this knower will consciously strive to background her own self in an attempt at reducing the effects of her own biases and expectations. Through this backgrounding, she may be able to foreground the other person and the world the latter inhabits. This backgrounding may have another effect too: it may lead our relational knower to be skeptical of standardized renditions of world philosophies. But what difference would this attitude make to knowledge about world philosophies? Let us take two examples: the terms "Islamic philosophy" and "Indian philosophy."

How Islamic Is Islamic Philosophy? Presentist Concerns and Knowledge Making

As noted by scholars of religion like Aaron Hughes (2013), Muslims living in different epochs and sociocultural spaces have been able to fashion their own distinctive identities using the heterogeneity of the tradition as a guide. And yet, given the larger geopolitical setup of our own times, and the role of Islam as an "other" in it, scholarship, in general, fails to discern the overlapping local interpretations of Islam that have been fleshed out in these identity processes. Rather, there seems to be a tendency in academic study to present Islam as a closed entity that moves effortlessly through time, space, and place. The active shaping, reshaping, performance, and contestation of various historical actors in the making of Muslim identities is overshadowed; we are presented with monolithic, "authentic Islamic" voices. But as Hughes rightly argues, the "use of words such as 'authenticity' should alert us that a value judgement is taking place" (2013: 10). That we are—in the process—dealing with reified versions of Islam is often lost from view. These thoughts seem to parallel developments in the field carved out as "Islamic philosophy."

Arguably, one fault line of the hitherto prevalent approach in Islamic studies and Islamic philosophy (and not only there; see below) seems to be the purportedly clean-cut division between "outsider-critics" and "insider-caretakers." In order to deliver "critical," "disinterested," "objective" scholarship, scholars are encouraged to take up, and maintain, the perspective of an outsider who does not actively participate in Islamic practices—however the latter are understood. Insiders, that is, participants in Islamic practices—however they are understood—are considered to be somehow "incompetent to function as scholars of their own tradition" (2013: 6). The worry is that—due to their close connection to the tradition—they would most likely deliver apologetic accounts of confessionalism under the guise of scholarship (cf. Gutas 2002: 19). Hughes seeks to bridge this so-called emic–etic divide by seeking a synthesis of the "caretaker's sensitivity with the critic's analytic rigor" (Hughes 2013: 6).

However, the history of philosophy in the Islamic world illustrates that a clean divide between outsider-critics and insider-caretakers is not feasible. A clear distinction between actors who worked to shape the inheritance of this tradition and scholars working to represent it cannot be strictly upheld. Not all philosophers in this tradition were practicing Muslims; in fact, some were not even believers in any religious denomination. Furthermore, many did not simply defer to religious injunctions (see Druart 2004: 116). Rather, they made extensive use of demonstrative reasoning, and they perceived themselves as interlocutors in an ongoing dialogue about topics of philosophical significance.

Scholars like Dimitri Gutas would not only underscore that the practitioners who shaped this tradition came from different backgrounds. Much like Gutas they would call out the general "biased orientalist attitude" of scholarship in the field (2002: 21), which has played a crucial role in sustaining the label "Islamic Philosophy." In his view, a more apt substitute would be "Arabic Philosophy," which is to say, philosophy composed in the Arabic language. As he notes: "Arabic was the language of Islamic civilization and the vehicle in which the identity and self-consciousness of that culture was cultivated and transmitted to all citizens in the Islamic world, regardless of their religion" (2002: 17).

Gutas hopes that such a radical renaming will be able to initiate a shift in the disciplinary ethos too such that "Arabic Philosophy" will be perceived to be what it really is: philosophy and not "confessionalism" under the guise of "scholarship" (2002: 19). This is not an abstract concern: the relational knower—as student, researcher, and teacher of "world philosophies"—must navigate these terminological concerns when she names her classes, when she declares her specializations in job interviews, when she publishes her work, and so forth. Will she select a term that is familiar within the mainstream, hence ensuring that she is understandable to journals, hiring committees, and undergraduates perusing the course catalog? Or will she select a term that makes an important disciplinary intervention while risking to remain invisible to those very mainstream members of the discipline that she seeks to influence?

The situation is even more complicated, given that Gutas's radical suggestion does not seem to be shared across the board. Thérèse-Anne Druart, for example, points out that the term "Arabic Philosophy" is not free of difficulties either, since not all the salient texts of the tradition were written in Arabic. Some important texts like those of Avicenna (Abū-ʿAlī al-Ḥusayn ibn-ʿAbdallāh Ibn-Sīnā ca. 970–1037) were penned by him in Persian. "Besides, the word *Arabic* may be construed as referring not only to the language used by the philosophers, but also to their ethnic background" (2004: 98). The term "Arabic Philosophy" would thus mark out the field by excluding, even if inadvertently, important texts and thinkers. In the process, it would lead to further misconceptions of a field, which in any case struggles to come to terms with its internal diversity. These considerations lead Druart to suggest that terms like "Philosophy in Islam" or "Philosophy in the Islamic World" be used instead of "Islamic Philosophy" or "Arab Philosophy." Often, as relational knowers seek to navigate the complex and overlapping dilemmas of terminological choices, the names of things become longer—some would say "clunkier"—and risk the appearance of pedantry.

Moreover, when we do not use terms that speak to a broad audience today, we run the additional risk of resigning philosophy to "intellectual history" and hence diminishing its power to speak to us here and now. For example, the presentist concerns voiced by historians of philosophy like Gutas and Druart will probably be shared by Nader El-Bizri. This philosopher observes how studies in philosophy of the Islamic world today are largely restricted to the *falsafa*, a tradition, which is largely considered to be a creative assimilation of Greek Peripatetic, Platonist, Neoplatonist, and Neo-Pythagorean positions by Islamicate authors, meaning authors working within the sociohistorical complex associated with Islam. In these studies, *falsafa* sources are typically examined in an archival mode as if they were disconnected from our own present-day philosophical world. "The historian of ideas,"

El-Bizri writes, "studies the intellectual history of Islam in the spirit of an antiquarian compiler of knowledge who reports the textual material, and endeavors to document it, in order to primarily serve the establishment of library references" (2010: 6). But this is not all. The merit of authors subsumed under the *falsafa* tradition is judged on the basis of a relatively simplistic scale: Can they "facilitate the pedagogic and intellectual understanding of European scholasticism, the mediaeval interpretation of the Greek corpus in general, and the Aristotelian tradition in particular?" (2010: 6).

Resisting such a simplistic and archival mode of inquiry, El-Bizri seeks to reset scholarship so that a new *falsafa* tradition can be initiated. The latter would be more conscious of the contemporaneity of our being, while also not severing the connection with its predecessor. But why bother to hammer out a "*falsafa* 2.0" version at all? El-Bizri (2016: 302) grounds his suggestion for a "neo-*falsafa*" with the following hermeneutic observation: even inherited texts are understood and interpreted through our own particular sociohistorical contexts. Texts are rendered meaningful to us through these webs of meaning. We relate them to "our epistemic preoccupations, cognitive frames of mind and embodiment as subjects with others in the world" (2016: 308).

In other words: El-Bizri prods us on to become more aware of how such particular, presentist prejudices drive our philosophical inquiry, even though we claim to engage in it dispassionately and objectively. Just as he would not subscribe to a rigid distinction between possessive caretakers and objective critics, El-Bizri would argue that a combination of the caretaker's sensitivity and the critic's analytic rigor has to be cultivated if we seek to adequately understand our own place in the philosophical world today.

Most places of academic learning in the world use a highly similar eurocentric philosophical canon. In general, this seems to be the case even in countries influenced by the Islamic tradition. As a result of this bias in academic philosophy, philosophers connected to Islam are led to paper over the cleavages resulting from their "multiple intellectual loyalties" and "aporetic antimonies" (2016: 306). In a bold attempt at taking back philosophy in the Islamic world and making it meaningful for our world today, El-Bizri appeals mainly to philosophers of multiple loyalties to boldly refract positions from this tradition through this "liminal region of the in-between" such that this tradition can become a fount of philosophical orientation for us and our multiple communities today (2010: 8, 10).

In general, as authors of this book, and series editors of the *Bloomsbury Introductions to World Philosophies*, we find ourselves aligning with projects, such as El-Bizri's "neo-*falsafa*," which ground themselves in indigenous terminology while speaking to contemporary concerns, without naively assuming to turn back the (colonial) clock, as it were, to a supposedly "authentic" core tradition. Such commitments underlie our choices of terms such as "Ruism" over "Confucianism" (as discussed in Chapter 2) and other decisions we made in the process of composing this book. That said, for any given relational knower navigating any given book, article, course syllabus, or job interview, there are no perfect answers but potentially many different ways of dealing with the dilemmas posed by terminological choices in the study of "world philosophies." The same or even similar solutions may not work across all contexts. We turn next to the emerging systematic debate on the viability of the term "Indian philosophy," which is yet in the early stages.

What Is Indian about Indian Philosophy? Inheritance and Representation

Typically, Indian philosophy is taught by subdividing it into six orthodox and three heterodox systems (*darśanas*). The main demarcation line is said to run between those systems that believed in the authority of the Vedas and those that did not. But as several authors point out, the manner in which Indian philosophy is presented today reflects a particular stage in the writing of European intellectual history and a stratification that is "borrowed from a history of European ideas" (Ganeri 2017: 4). This writing has, in addition, "tended toward obsessive interest in a select few individuals" to use an observation made by Jonardon Ganeri (2017: 2) The categories used hereby arose during complex processes of European self-identification and self-positioning in the nineteenth and twentieth centuries. Despite the specificity of this writing of history and its embeddedness in a particular locale, scholarship in philosophy has only recently begun to reflect on the adequacy of its organizing categories.

In the wake of detailed studies on doxography by the likes of Wilhelm Halbfass (1940–2000) and Andrew J. Nicholson, we know today that the boundaries between the "orthodox" and "heterodox" systems were blurry and changed through time. From an immanent perspective, even schools like the Advaita Vedānta, whose orthodox pedigree are taken at face value today, were considered to be heretical and (thus heterodox) by the likes of the polymath Vijñanabhikśu in Sanskritic India (Nicholson 2011: 180). Read against this light, terms like "orthodox" and "heterodox" merely reflect one particular (later) stage in these internal debates. Studying such local doxographies (*saṃgraha*), Nicholson suggests that the terms *āstika* and *nāstika*, for which "orthodoxy" and "heterodoxy" are respectively taken as placeholders, may be misleading (2011: 178). Depending on the context, "affirmers" and "deniers" would be a more appropriate way of understanding the Sanskrit terminology.

As Nicholson illustrates, we could foreground important differences in the local context by achieving a better fit between the concepts we use and local practices. Philosophers in Sanskritic India, for example, did not attempt to offer a catalog of all extant schools in their writing. Rather, they used idealized and abstract renditions of important extant scholarship to position their own schools in distinctive ways, as often being the best possible alternative to metaphysical problems, in the form of a manuscript-culture akin to the one we encountered in Chapter 2. Endorsing such a fine-grained analysis of these local debates, he directs our attention to how even the act of writing a philosophy is doing philosophy. "Even when this is not explicit there are always implicit philosophical commitments that the historian of philosophy brings to bear on her subjects, including philosophical commitments about the nature of history itself" (2011: 21).

To achieve a better fit between concepts we use and local practices, we need scholarship that emphasizes "regionality, vernaculars, subaltern communities, eccentrics, [an exploration] of scholarly networks, nodes of philosophical activity, transnational encounters, and contexts of philosophical invention" (Ganeri 2017: 2). By including such scholarship in the curriculum on Indian philosophy, we may begin to end the long history of exclusion of Indian philosophy from professional philosophy in Europe and North America. As is well known, the purportedly religious, non-secular attempts of such systems at overcoming this life through *mokṣa* were dismissed as being at odds with the reason-based bent of standard academic philosophy. More generally, they were considered to be incapable of pursuing theory for theory's sake, a supposed hallmark of academic philosophy in Europe (see Chapter 2). If they had any philosophical merit at all, then only as historical precursors to modern, European academic philosophy. Drawing on James Madaio's observations in a related context, we can say that this exclusion has resulted through a privileging of certain periods over others, demarcating periods of "philosophical flourishing" from others and through a marginalization of certain text genres over others (2017: 101). This tradition of exclusion is largely continued. Only recently have specialists in Indian philosophy begun to find placements in philosophy departments in North America and the United Kingdom.

As we see, there is no plausible reason not to move away from the standard representation of *darśanic* Indian philosophy. The presentation of the subject, which arose during a particular time in European colonial expansion, does merit a critical examination before it is continued in today's postcolonial context. Fine-grained analyses of the intellectual history of the Indian subcontinent could be implemented to initiate a more critical debate on the category "Indian philosophy" itself. Why should schools and positions that are spread out across the subcontinent (and in other parts of Asia) be grouped together today under the name of India, a nation-state? What unique grounds, one could ask, make the political territory of this state the best lens through which to capture the plurality of traditions, most of which did not even include its framing in their self-identification? Furthermore, if India is the best qualifier for this tradition, does the term "Indian philosophy" include all the traditions found within its political territory today?

Arguably, some important philosophers living under coloniality did underscore that their own traditions were otherworldly and spiritual. They were proud that their traditions did not engage in "logic-chopping for its own sake" (Daya Krishna 1986: 64). This narrative could be continued after political independence too, partly because the unification of India as a nation was tied up with this supposedly unique spiritual legacy.[1] Today, we can contest the narrative of India's unique spiritual legacy with the help of contemporary philosophical resources. Take for example Krishnachandra Bhattacharya's (1875–1949) famous call for cultivating an independence (*svarāj*) in ideas.

In his "Svaraj in Ideas," a lecture held in 1931 and published posthumously, Bhattacharya endeavored to navigate a special place for philosophy in what has been called the Indian renaissance. Bhattacharya (1984 [1931]: 383) warned about a "cultural subjection," which leads to a "slavery of the spirit." Having imbibed "western culture," Bhattacharya saw his contemporaries as peering "into our ancient culture as a curiosity and with the attitude of foreign oriental scholars" (1984 [1931]: 384). They do not, in general, want to know or care to know "this indigenous nature of ours." And if they do, he reasons, they do not feel that "they are discovering their own self." An intellectual apathy has resulted; the "Indian mind" "has subsided below the level of culture." Bhattacharya calls upon his audience to shake off the scales from their eyes, and experience "a rebirth, . . . a Svaraj in ideas" (1984 [1931]: 383). For this purpose, "certain habits of soulless thinking, which appear like real thinking" have to be discarded (1984 [1931]: 385); an independence of thought has to be relearnt.

To achieve this independence, one must, he argues, become aware and palpably feel the hiatus between bookish knowledge imbibed in British educational institutions and the sociopolitical reality of his contemporary India. Bhattacharya was especially worried about the outcome of the general apathy and lack of creativity in the field of philosophy: "It is in philosophy, if anywhere, that the task of discovering the soul of India is imperative for the modern India; the task of, if possible, achieving the continuity of his old self with his present day self, of realising what is nowadays called the Mission of India, if it has any" (1984 [1931]: 386–7). Only adequate concepts, which are generated after a proper "synthesis of Indian thought with western thought," would help one judge whether there is such a mission after all (1984 [1931]: 384). "[N]ational conceit and unthinking glorification of everything in our culture" are not viable options (1984 [1931]: 391), he cautioned.

Importantly, Bhattacharya highlights that such a synthesis should not be taken to be a "patchwork of ideas of different cultures" achieved through a mere assimilation of alien ideas (1984 [1931]: 388). Furthermore, synthesis is not a general universal trick-box. Only some contexts warrant it. And: "Where it is demanded, the foreign ideal has to be assimilated to our ideal, and not the other way. There is no demand for the surrender of our individuality in any case" (1984 [1931]: 389). Only an attitude of "critical reserve" of "infinite patience and humility" would help navigate one through this process of careful evaluation (1984 [1931]: 390, 392). But why synthesis?

For Bhattacharya, the universality of reason is not a fixed, *a priori* principle, simply waiting to be implemented. Reason cannot simply slice through space and time. It has to be vernacularized, hammered out in different languages, by groups who perceive themselves as being committed to upholding this universality. Only then "can we think productively on our own account" (1984 [1931]: 393).

As we see, Bhattacharya's normative project encompasses all actors of the public sphere, including those who being involved in the marketplace of ideas claim to be guided by the call of reason. He singles out philosophers for this task because by virtue of their profession, they should in his reasoning realize that ideas and ideals are joined at the hip, so to speak. Ideals can only be materialized through ideas; ideas for their part have to be guided by ideals. Bhattacharya's insistence on a skeptical attitude and critical reserve toward extant narratives as well as on the use of adequate concepts seems to warrant an inquiry into the adequacy of the term "Indian philosophy." This position might receive support from someone, who in the history of the subcontinent is said to have carried some weight in the creation of India's neighbor, Pakistan: Muhammad Iqbal (1877–1938).

"Modern knowledge is the greatest blind— / Idol-worshipping, idol-selling, idol-making! / Shackled in the prison of phenomena / It has not overleaped the limits of the sensible" (1920: 129). These words of Iqbal echo in some ways Bhattacharya's call for a philosophy on the Indian subcontinent, which first feels the hiatus between European philosophy and sociopolitical practice, and then strives to bridge it through adequate concepts. Iqbal's *Reconstruction of Religious Thought in Islam* warns that "the world is not something to be merely seen or known through concepts, but something to be made and re-made by continuous action" (1954 [1934]: 198). Accordingly, philosophical activity on the subcontinent cannot be restricted to a mere application of concepts made elsewhere. Concepts have to arise out of a reflection about concrete, local experience.

In his philosophical writings, Iqbal strove to find a "more fundamental 'I am,'" whose fundamentality and consistency could be tested in action. Passive imitation, whether of philosophical concepts made elsewhere or of "ancient customs" would dissolve the ego instead of strengthening it. This is why "idols of tribe and caste" have to be broken deliberately. "True doctrine" cannot be understood in the quibbling of "seventy-two sects." It is impossible "to understand it if your perception is not impartial" (quoted in Diagne 2010: 31, 32).[2] For a Sufi like him, this meant that "the ego needs to renew its contact with the very source of time, the one that makes it into a factor that participates in life in the universe" (2010: 23).

Iqbal too endorsed an independent but "respectful" engagement with "modern knowledge" which would enable one to "appreciate the teachings of Islam in the light of that knowledge, even though we may be led to differ from those who have gone before us" (1954 [1934]: 97). And just like Bhattacharya, Iqbal warned about a simplistic synthesis. Take for example "liberal ideas in Islam." Liberalism in his view had a tendency to "act as a force of disintegration." As a result, "the race-idea which appears to be working in modern Islam with greater force than ever may ultimately wipe off the board human outlook which Muslim people have imbibed from their religion" (1954 [1934]: 162–3). Bhattacharya's and Iqbal's endorsement of a philosophy grounded in practice would be seconded in today's India by authors working on "Dalit theory" (Satyanarayana 2013).[3]

Gopal Guru's call for a Dalit theory is based on his observation that Indian academia is split up into the "theoretical pundits who are 'theoretical Brahmins'" in the system and the "inferior mass of academics" who are the system's "empirical Shudras" (Guru and Sarukkai 2012: 10–11). As members of the highest erstwhile caste hierarchy, Brahmins dominate theory production in the social sciences in India and elsewhere, while Shudras, members of the erstwhile lowest ranks of this hierarchy, engage in empirical work, or write poetry. With this division of labor, erstwhile caste privilege for the Brahmins is kept intact.

In Guru's analysis, Dalits admit that they have a unique access to their own social reality. However, they shy away from doing theory since this makes "a person intellectually arrogant, egoistic and socially alienated" from the group (2012: 23). If, however, Dalits, says Guru, took up their "social responsibility to do theory," they would be able to "restore agency" (2012: 24) for themselves. Why so? For Guru, only theory "demands clarity of concept and principles and the open examination of one's own action to see whether it is justified" (Guru 2012: 23). By actively doing theory, Dalits as a group would be able to one day develop and implement a vision of an alternative future for themselves. He, thus, calls upon fellow Dalits to develop an "enduring moral stamina," which is necessary to engage in theory (2012: 21). Poetry cannot be enough for this marginalized group since it "has no conceptual capacity to universalize the particular and particularize the universal" (2012: 23).

The reasoning here seems to be in some respects similar to that of the Indigenous philosophers we encountered in Chapter 3: a viable conception of transformative politics for Dalits as an oppressed and marginalized group should be grounded in a theory, which has developed out of the concrete experiences this group has had. A sociopolitical transformation (for this group and through it, larger society) can take place only when (social) theory has been enriched by the experiences of this group. A mere application of extant theoretical concepts to the Dalit situation will not suffice. One reason being that absent these experiences of oppression and marginalization, these theoretical accounts will not be able to track them. These experiences will not be captured by theory's hermeneutical shortcomings. To "communicate the unified nature of social experience," presupposes that a "theoretical mediation of differentiated experience" is possible (2012: 119).

Notably, Guru does not endorse a theory that delimits its universality. Rather, he envisages an active involvement of different societal groups in theory production. In India, this theory production would involve Dalits, who till date continue to play a relatively marginal role in this activity. Theorizing about their own lived experiences in public, Dalits would be able to engage with others about the marginalization and oppression they face. Using theoretical tools, both sides would be able to develop a more nuanced discussion about sociopolitical reality in India today.

Guru's critical intervention has led to a larger debate about theory production in India today. While some are skeptical about the status of a "felt-ontology" (Gurukkal 2013) in theory-making, others question whether an integration of Dalits into theory production can in any way alleviate their situation. A. Raghuramaraju appeals to an "ethics of care" to argue that Dalit scholars like Guru should not attempt to "move" Dalits from poetry into theory for a particular reason: eurocentric theoretical models, which are in play in Indian academia, systematically stymie the entry of people from the "non-west" into theory. In addition, these models are geared to "only process the rationalistic, cognitive experience of the techno-capital global world" (2010: 164). They will thus be blind to the lived experiences of Dalits. Guru's vision of a Habermasian-inspired Dalit theory will most likely lead to a dead-end for Dalits because models like those of Habermas are "obsessively self-centered" (2010: 167). This analysis leads Raghuramaraju to propose that non-Dalit academics, who now control theory production, move to the spaces their Dalit peers already inhabit, like those of poetry. In order to create a more level-playing field with, and for, Dalits, the conversation about their asymmetrical status in Indian academia should be conducted in spaces in which Dalits are at ease.

In some ways, our discussion so far echoes some aspects of Jitendranath Mohanty's ruminations on the topic. Mohanty prefers to use the term "Indian philosophy" for "any philosophical work which self-consciously takes up that core-tradition, and *perceives itself as continuing* the discussion of the *themes, issues* and *problems* formulated in, and arising out of, that tradition, no matter in what language and irrespective of the geographical and socio-political loyalty of the author" (1982: 235; emphasis in original). By focusing on themes, issues, and problems, Mohanty seeks to redraw the boundary of Indian philosophy such that it can include non-Indian scholars of the field too. The Indianness of Indian philosophy cannot be restricted in his view to scholarship by people of Indian descent only (1982: 235).

Arguably, Mohanty's decided attempt to redraw this boundary does not extend very far: his discussion about core texts and their interpretations in the aforementioned quote could be read as reinforcing the standard *darśanic* rendition of Indian philosophy. This impression could be strengthened when one takes into account that the essay does not tease out whether—and how—one could philosophize outside the standard framework set by the *darśana*s. Notwithstanding this gap, Mohanty seems to clearly advocate a radical questioning about philosophy's very fundament:

> For, whereas in the context of other sorts of systems (mathematical, and even cultural) genuine criticism is internal, it appears to be repugnant to the spirit of *philosophy* to limit criticism to the internal standards of a system. Nothing intrinsic to philosophizing can stop it from being radical questioning, i.e. questioning the basic pre-suppositions including the historical-cultural accomplishments. Thus, there is, in the very nature of philosophizing, a universality which one ignores, if one restricts it to the parameters of the *darśana*-tradition, as much as if one restricts it, as many western thinkers tend to do, to those of the *philosophia*-tradition. (1982: 241; emphasis in original)

In the Classroom: Terminological Choices and Philosophical Practice

Here we turn to the topic of how the questions about terminological choices in the naming of "world philosophies" affect our practices as professionals in the classroom and other academic institutional spaces. As discussed in Chapter 2, the eurocentric philosophical canon shapes our contemporary departmental cultures on multiple fronts. For example, the curricular requirements for the major and minor most often include a standard "history of philosophy" series that recapitulates Kantian historiography from "ancient Greece" to "modern Europe." Our course catalogs, for another example, reflect familiar categories that are the products of European philosophy's disciplinary schema, such as metaphysics, ethics, logic, and epistemology. When we send students to graduate school, they learn to discuss their specializations in terms of this intellectual history and these disciplinary categories. When they enter the job market, they answer job ads that are seeking specialists similarly defined by this history and categorization.

Imagine for a moment an undergraduate philosophy department shaped by different terms. Instead of "ancient philosophy" and "modern philosophy," students have taken classes in Han-dynasty philosophy and Song-dynasty philosophy—the appropriate historical markers for discussing important moments in Chinese intellectual history. Instead of analytic philosophy and continental philosophy, students have been taught buddha-dharma (*fofa* 佛法) and the Ru-lineage (*rujia* 儒家), reflecting two of the major competing approaches in China to fundamental questions regarding selves, worlds, and ways of knowing. Finally, instead of epistemology and ethics, students have been taught to distinguish "*li*-studies" (*lixue* 理學) from "*xin*-studies" (*xinxue* 心學), two major Ruist disciplinary categories that emerged during the Song period. It goes without saying that any student trained in this way would be unrecognizable to graduate programs or hiring committees.

The problem is not just that such philosophers would be using foreign terms unfamiliar in mainstream philosophy today. The problem is that the very terms and categories place our hypothetical student outside the bounds of philosophy "proper" and somewhere within area studies, religious studies, or perhaps the discipline of history. Let us return to the question of the Dalit scholar discussed earlier. On the one hand, we recognize the problematic fact that "theories" and "methods" tend to be derived from eurocentric sources and then applied to a diverse array of "topics" and "areas of study," which may include, for example, Asian, African, or Indigenous traditions.[4] From this perspective, it is empowering to say that Dalit scholars can and should be theorists, not poets. Moreover, it is progressive to consider theories and methods derived from non-eurocentric sources (like the Chinese *li*-studies mentioned earlier, which is certainly a viable scholarly method, albeit one difficult to capture in European philosophical categories).

On the other hand, does this very emphasis on theory above aesthetic expression not already uphold the classic European philosophical prejudice against emotion for the sake of reason? Or, when we, along with a scholar like Bhattacharya, attempt to recover the (spiritual) legacy of Indian thought and resist the sterile logic-chopping of the European tradition, do we not thereby reinscribe stereotypes regarding the rational "West" and the mystical "East"? In a sense, by walking away from the standard terms and categories of mainstream philosophy today, we risk affirming the very prejudices we seek to subvert.

We return to our earlier comment that there are no perfect solutions but a multitude of acceptable approaches to navigating these various dilemmas of "world philosophies." Moreover, we suggest that the dilemmas themselves are pedagogically instructive and should be invited into the practice of philosophy at the undergraduate level. We offer again an example taken from our own classrooms.

For a final assignment, students were asked to design their own "dream department" in world philosophies. They constructed a website for this imagined department, complete with separate webpages for the departmental mission statement, a course catalog of required and elective courses, and the curricular requirements for the major and minor. The challenge was to craft a coherent program of study for the diversity of "world philosophies."

For example, students had to decide how to conceive of and explain "diversity" itself. Should this mean requiring classes that reflect a variety of geographical regions (i.e., with courses titled European philosophy or African philosophy)? Or, should diversity instead be understood along linguistic or intellectual-historical lines (as in the transregional scope of courses such as Philosophy in the Islamic World or Buddhist Philosophy)? Or, yet again, might diversity be understood via a topics-centered approach that organizes curricular content around certain grounding themes (like the "selves," "worlds," and "ways of knowing" of our own book)? The students quickly found that any given approach came with its own set of pros and cons. Yet, along with that, they developed the thoughtfulness and patience required to navigate the complex, interlocking issues uniting the question of the disciplinary practice of philosophy to the global history of coloniality and imperialism. By inviting students to become our partners in this venture, we can together come to celebrate the fact that there is no "neutral" position. How we choose to "do" philosophy in the relational network of the classroom reflects ongoing and fluctuating power dynamics, which establish the marginalized and the mainstream within specific local contexts, such that what is empowering in one context may be problematic in another. But, this is another way to say that philosophy is an active and constructive endeavor, that it helps us articulate complex dilemmas, and that with that articulation comes the possibility of growth and progress. In the classroom situation, we can work out with students why there is merit in not being led by the standard narrative that philosophy is—and must be—static and teleological (see the discussion in Chapter 3).

Conclusion: Moving Forward

Moving alongside our relational knower into the worlds of philosophy in Islam and in the Indic traditions has alerted us to the possibility that labels like "Islamic philosophy" or "Indian philosophy" that we routinely use in scholarship and in the classroom may be convenient heuristics but are problematic nevertheless. Philosophical traditions are presented herein as "a passive happening (impersonal)," "or as a noun (reified)," but not "as an act (discoursing)" (Sjödin 2011: 541). The labels suggest homogenized and unchanging traditions of the past, which are far removed from our own philosophical endeavors.

If we—alongside our relational knower—seek to engage with the worlds of philosophy relationally, we may have to muster up the courage to depart from at least some cherished bits of furniture that we have hitherto used to set up our philosophical home. We may have to open ourselves up to the possibility that the windows of our own philosophical home are not the only apertures on to the world outside. Specific events in world history may just have led up to them.

As several authors warn us, "European colonialism enabled a whole network of European categories, ideas and paradigms to appear more universal and normative than they might have otherwise seemed" (King 2009: 38). Backed up by colonial power, only one way of knowing was universalized through time. Today, the "deafening silence" (2009: 39) in mainstream philosophical debates about globalization, colonialism, and capitalism may not necessarily be an indication of the intellectual superiority of European and Euro-American categories, ideas, and paradigms. Rather, they may just reflect the role academic philosophy in Europe has played in "making sure that any foreigners crossing the border are properly classified as 'religious' rather than 'philosophical'" (2009: 44). Wherever we are located today, our standard conceptions of doing philosophy still, it seems, reflect the exercise of that power. We seem to be gripped in the discipline by what some thinkers call "global coloniality." The eurocentric setup of academic philosophy goes to the very roots of our discipline. As Rivera notes: "Eurocentrism is not a derivative character of modern Western philosophy; it, rather, comes to define how Western philosophy articulates the systems of knowledge and truth that characterize it" (2019: 105).

It would be rash, and self-defeating, to claim that extant bodies of rich research bundled neatly under the labels "Islamic philosophy," "Indian philosophy," "Chinese philosophy," "Japanese philosophy," or "Latin American philosophy" should be abandoned without further ado. Rather, as our discussion highlights, we have reason to be skeptical about how many of those tightly knit bundles were said to be irrelevant to understanding our place in the world here and now. In addition, we have grounds to become more aware about the contingent nature of such labels and their homogenizing power in directing future research. The aforementioned branches of philosophy arose to a large extent through the use of eurocentric paradigms. As a result, only those bits of these traditions were mapped "that happen within the universal" (2019: 106). Others that did not match the template were excluded. One created a single world of philosophy in which one universal European center drew up several peripheries, be they uniquely Islamic, Indian, Chinese, Japanese, or Latin American.

To move forward, we may need to step back to pause. As we hope the pedagogical discussion in this chapter illustrates, we can and should invite our students to take this pause with us. Together we may then be able to bring to mind academic philosophy's commitment to critical thinking and love of wisdom. Pausing to reflect about this commitment, would perhaps nudge us all to double-check whether the current practices of our discipline can, and do in fact, live up to its guiding ideals.

Discussion Questions

- What could "structural prejudices" be? Can you come up with a few examples?
- What does a "hegemonic theory production" mean to you? What would its opposite? How would an alternative theory production be achieved?
- Are there reasons for involving societal groups in the making of theory?
- Would a delimitation of criticism be repugnant to the spirit of philosophy in your view? If so, why?
- If we are all gripped by "global coloniality" would there be a way out at all? What ways would such a philosophizing take?

Conclusion

Generations of comparative philosophers have worked to integrate world-philosophical traditions into the academy. Typically, they have been content with (or have had to resort to) applying eurocentric theory to non-European and non-Euro-American material. To this end, some of them have mined other traditions for solutions to problems that standard paradigms in mainstream philosophy raise. Despite all this, such work nonetheless tends to privilege eurocentric theory as the default position from which *all* issues of philosophical relevance are gauged. As we saw in Chapter 3, one role assigned to world-philosophical source material is that it is implemented to fill in lacunae in dominant theory. This source material is used in other contexts to underscore the cultural superiority of the European narrative, as noted in Chapter 4. Notably, not everyone in the field is on board with this way of engaging with world philosophies.

Writing about environmental ethics in 1987, Gerald Larson was concerned about how comparative philosophers attempted to fill in the "need" for the "increasing 'demand' for some new intellectual commodities" (1987: 151). In his analysis, this way of doing comparative philosophy entailed a commitment to "external appropriation" in which "[i]deas and concepts come to be construed as 'things' or 'entities' that can be disembedded from their appropriate frameworks and then processed and made to fit into our own frameworks. Such a method for comparative philosophy is . . . one-dimensional, overly selective, forced, anachronistic, sociologically unsophisticated, and, perhaps, worst of all, unpersuasive" (1987: 153). Today, we can better understand why comparative philosophers must explore the myriad ramifications of their methodological choices.

As we have seen in Chapters 3, 4, and 5, part of the problem has to do with an inattentiveness to the social dimension of philosophizing. Without sufficiently attending to the ways in which their own positionality colors attempts to understand world philosophies, standard approaches in comparative philosophy run the risk of simply presupposing that the conceptual apparatus of eurocentric theory can accurately track philosophy in other cultural contexts. In other words, they risk working as if methodologies derived from European and Euro-American sources are indeed able to deliver true and accurate representations of "Asian philosophy," "Latin American philosophy," "African philosophy," but also "Indian philosophy," "Chinese philosophy," "Japanese philosophy," and so on. Such an approach would fail to see how these methods, in their own ways, replicate the racialized understanding of philosophy.

What evidence of this racialized understanding can we see in comparative philosophy today? In a 2007 essay David H. Kim asks the deceptively simple question: Why has comparative philosophy almost always been associated exclusively with "East-West" dialogue? He offers the deceptively simple answer: Hegel. As Kim explains:

> Whatever may be the full story of classical Asian philosophy's unique reception, I think it cannot have as its center the apparently innocent idea that early Western proponents of classical Asian philosophy simply understood and appreciated the special philosophical character and potential contributions of this foreign system of thought. . . . Whatever the full story might be, it seems difficult to plausibly deny here the long-standing reign of the Hegelian world-historical hierarchy in which it is believed that only the expressions of Asian civilizations begin to approach those of Europe. The turn toward Asia, it seems, was also a turn away from Africa and the indigenous Americas, among other places. Incidentally, the entrenchment of this Hegelian structure might help explain why, once admitted into philosophy proper, classical Asian philosophy, presumably stagnant or immature, was so often relegated to the margins. (2007: 222–4)[1]

On a quasi-Hegelian ranking of world civilizations, informed by the pseudoscience of "white," "black," "red," and "yellow" races, Europeans and Africans made up the two ends of the spectrum of philosophical ability. On this supposed spectrum, as Kim references, "Asian civilizations [began] to approach those of Europe" and thus had a relative ability to philosophize, the potential of which, however, they failed to fully explore. Echoes of this racialized hierarchy are still with us in cross-cultural philosophy in what Kim calls the "East-West paradigm" (2019: 42). This is to say, a majority of publication output, research, and teaching in comparative philosophy, especially in North America, is dedicated to philosophies associated with Asia. It is precisely a situation such as this with which comparativists today must reckon.

Chapters 2 and 4 have delivered ample reasons for not falling in line with the "politics of purity" that a racialized model insinuates. This politics of purity renders its own positionality invisible by appealing "to fixed states, abstracted and idealized agents, and rigid application of rules and procedures" (Monahan 2011: 222). Driven by an instrumental understanding of reason, this account claims that only it can help us organize and master "discrete units of knowledge that can then be exchanged in a free market of ideas" (2011: 216). But this understanding of reason is counterintuitive. Its suggestion that these processes are the culmination of what reason can ever achieve, ironically, renders us passive bystanders in the name of thinking, who can at best only rehearse the heights of reason soared in Europe's past. To do so, we must strictly obey the rules of the game set by a group of thinkers, who were either Europeans or North Americans of European descent. This methodological foreclosure through which a particular group of philosophers have established "themselves as the sole arbiters of a purified (and reified) notion of genuine philosophy" flies in the face of thinking itself (2011: 211). It is difficult to understand why the ability to philosophize can only have been gifted to one exclusive group in one relatively recent segment of human history. That the truth of this claim is itself bracketed from further philosophical inquiry should make us even more skeptical about its plausibility.

As we have seen in Chapter 1, an increasing number of philosophers and scholars are dissatisfied with their "own reflection in disguise" revealed by the standard eurocentric conceptual schemes deployed in comparative work (Rosenlee 2006: 3). Deliberately moving away from these conceptual schemes, they invite us to join them in their deliberate acts of epistemic disobedience through which philosophy can be opened up to "myriad kinds of human becoming" (Monahan 2011: 222). In the name of reason itself, they call for "a change in attitude to the diversity of theory and practice" (Ram-Prasad 2018: 23). Guided by the belief that "questions about what humans are should be communicable, interpretable, and understandable conceptually across the specific cultural boundaries that the contingencies of history have thrown up" (Ram-Prasad 2018: 185), they call upon the field to reconsider the self-image of academic philosophy as an undertaking bereft of any cultural moorings. In fact, like any other human endeavor, philosophy is steeped through and through with the way we human beings make meanings of our own selves and our places in the world through exchanges with our communities.

Philosophers engaging in epistemic disobedience work on several fronts to open up the field to more plural ways of human becoming. Some attempt to historicize professional philosophy as we know and practice it today to underscore how the discipline's claims to universality are themselves historically embedded. Others engage with genres typically taken to fall outside the remit of professional philosophy to illustrate their significance to our philosophical undertakings. Yet others seek to develop mindful practices that can make us understand the shortcomings of the adversarial method prevalent in academic philosophy (Mattice 2014). Cultivating these practices, we would be able to discard the politics of purity that are prevalent in our professional lives. In different ways, these paths lead to a judicious study of world philosophies, meaning views of the world stemming from different intellectual and cultural traditions. They destabilize the temporal positioning of the conventional view about philosophical thinking, while highlighting that philosophical thinking's "imagined architectures do not abide by single temporal horizons" (Rivera 2019: 174).

Our series *Bloomsbury Introductions to World Philosophies* intends to bring together work that pluralizes our understanding of philosophy. Its easily accessible primers will seek to implement what Ganeri in another context has called a "pluralism about epistemic stances" (2019: 7). Stances are open-ended policies "adopted towards the employment of epistemic principles" (2019: 7). They do not dictate how epistemic principles should be applied to concrete situations. Rather, they make room for different routes to world philosophies such that these routes "collectively constitute 'a view from everywhere'" (2019: 9). We conclude by sharing a few thoughts on how we, as editors of the *Bloomsbury Introductions to World Philosophies*, have tried to make room for these diverse routes in our series.

Organizing a Series in Flux

The eurocentrism of mainstream philosophy is held in place at a structural level via the terminological choices that determine everything from our academic specializations, to the titles of our books and journals, to the organization of a book series such as ours. As editors of this series, we face dilemmas regarding the mapping of "world philosophies" and the marketing of our content to relevant audiences. In many cases, we walk a line between the desire to intervene in hegemonic practices and the need to remain visible and understandable within the mainstream academic discipline. Our experiences at this often-fuzzy border speak to larger issues related to "doing" philosophy via relational knowing.

In organizing the format for the *Bloomsbury Introductions to World Philosophies*, we strove to designate flexible categories and to contextualize their meaning. The series currently solicits titles related to seven major areas, each overseen by a regional editor, including African philosophy, Chinese philosophy, Indian philosophy, Indigenous philosophy, philosophy in the Islamicate world, Japanese philosophy, and Latin American philosophy. As is evident, this schema includes geographical, linguistic, and intellectual-historical categories. Some of the considerations that have guided our decision-making in this regard include (1) acknowledging and celebrating the political dimensions of certain category designations, (2) adhering to a schema that allows for ample cross-referencing and cross-categorization, and (3) adopting an organizational plan that remains open-ended and amenable to future modifications and additions.

Regarding the first consideration—that is, the political dimensions of various categories—we look at our area editorship in Indigenous philosophy as an illustrative example. At present, this category focuses on traditions in the Americas and Oceania, but the boundary of such a category is necessarily contested. As discussed in Chapter 4, the scope of the term "Indigenous" overlaps with regions typically categorized under the heading "primal" or "native" in many world religions textbooks; and, most problematically, these headings themselves are vestiges of older (and now quite inappropriate) designations such as "paganism," "heathenism," and "idolatry." And yet, as Chapter 4 also made clear, the field of Indigenous philosophy serves as a site of reclaimed power, where scholarship and activism intersect, and which contributes significantly to the methodological interventions in the practices of philosophy that we as editors prioritize.

Latin American philosophy is another such example of a tradition whose political context deeply informs its identity. In many ways, the tradition itself was born from a heritage of political critique and resistance, fostered by an active culture of political philosophy on the continent in the twentieth century. As such, some Latin American philosophers have been associated with various critical strands of European and Euro-American thought, such as Marxism, feminism, and so forth, as well as a concern for the specific neocolonial realities of the region. That said, Latin American philosophy is not necessarily about any of the precolonial traditions of Indigenous philosophy on the continent, such as Aztec or Mayan. This brings us to the second consideration that has guided our practice as editors of the Bloomsbury series—that is, the possibility for cross-referencing and cross-categorization. A given title in the series might be fruitfully categorized and marketed as a work in Latin American philosophy alone, or as a work in Indigenous philosophy alone, or cross-referenced under both categories. This capacity for cross-referencing helps us construct a more nuanced world of philosophies, so as to better capture the complexity of the relational networks that knit together diverse traditions.

Obviously, this construction is always in progress—it is an open-ended activity that can and should be able to respond flexibly to changing conditions. As such, the seven editorial areas we currently promote are not set in stone. New areas might be added in the future, or existing areas might be further sub-divided as needed. This relates to the last consideration that has guided our work as series editors—adopting an organizational plan that remains amenable to future modifications. All in all, our editorial work is a practice of the same relational knowing we have discussed in this book—a process of nuanced and complex contextualization that always demands of us further attention to detail, further conversation with others whose expertise in diverse areas educates us in our editorial decision-making, and further sensitivity to the changing conditions around us that require we continually revisit and revise our current practices.

Teaching Notes and Further Reading

Throughout the book, each chapter concludes with discussion questions related to the themes covered and suggestions for further conversation. We intend our "Teaching Notes" for classroom activities, assignments, and further readings to be useful to teachers who might consult our book in preparing class modules on world-philosophical content, or who might assign the book itself, or parts of it, to students.

Chapter 1

Chapter 1 lays the ground for a substantial methodological reorientation in the study of world philosophies. Teachers might use this chapter to draw attention to the infelicities of standard comparative approaches and to introduce new work that explicitly seeks to overcome these shortcomings. The chapter is an ideal place to begin a creative exploration of other formats and genres in teaching world philosophies.

Teaching Suggestions

- Use astronomical, cartographical, and other material to illustrate the fluidity of terms like "East," "West," "North," and "South." For example, show students images of the world map in the so-called south-up orientation (readily available online) and have them research the use of this map in various social and political contexts (see the C. Williams entry in suggestions for further reading below for an accessible BBC article). In a class on world philosophies, one might have students draw their own philosophical map of the world at the beginning and at the end of the term. At the end of the semester, encourage students to change the cardinal points they used in the first map. How does this change in their view alter their understanding of the world?

- Work with students to find poems, songs, paintings, social media, and so on, which can illustrate the open-ended nature of philosophizing in a world context. For example, in the context of the Chan (Zen) Buddhist tradition, one very famous philosophical debate over the meaning of enlightenment takes place via a poetry context, as described in the *Platform Sutra* of Huineng (cf. Yampolsky (trans.) 2012). Given Zen's overall suspicion of language as an appropriate tool for discussing ultimate reality, the use of poetry as a form of expression might be said to convey philosophical nuance that direct speech obscures. Have students discuss what the poems convey that ordinary speech cannot. Perhaps have them experiment with writing their own poetry as a means for expressing their philosophical ideas.
- To initiate a discussion of comparative methodologies, give students Paul Masson-Oursel's 1951 essay "True Philosophy Is Comparative Philosophy." Then, ask them to discuss whether Masson-Oursel's remarks about comparative methodologies do or do not address the concerns about eurocentrism raised here.

Further Reading

Chakrabarti, A. and Weber, R. (2016), "Introduction," in *Comparative Philosophy Without Borders*, 1–33, London and New York: Bloomsbury.

> A nuanced exposition of the problems that ensue with a "naked comparison." Claims that the epithet "comparative" will wither away; the field is moving toward "fusion philosophy," meaning,

"a smudging and tearing down of borders." Excerpts may come in handy to make students reflect on the adequacy of terms like "comparative philosophy," "fusion philosophy," and "world philosophies" at the end of the course.

Christian, B. (1987), "The Race for Theory," *Cultural Critique*, (6): 51–63.

Argues that theory has become a commodity through which academic hegemony is made and stabilized and that the center perpetuates itself through the commodification of academic labor.

Connolly, T. (2015), *Doing Philosophy Comparatively*, London: Bloomsbury.

Provides students with key vocabulary to define and discuss various methodologies related to the fields of comparative and cross-cultural philosophy. Prepares students to engage with some of the critical claims we make in Chapter 1 regarding the history of comparative methodologies and to better evaluate the distinctive features of what we refer to as our own world-philosophical approach.

Heisig, J. (2004), "The Place of Japanese Philosophy," *Japan Studies Review*, (8): 97–110.

Lucid introduction to problems which ensue through the use of binaries like "eastern spirituality" and "western rationality," despite using these terms himself. Urges one to include other voices in terms like "global human community." Easy to use in an "intro" class.

Maffie, J. (2009), "'In the End, We Have the Gatling Gun, and They Have Not': Future Prospects of Indigenous Knowledges," *Futures*, 41 (1): 53–65.

A widely read essay on a global polycentric epistemology that underscores the power dynamics at play in academic philosophy.

Smith, L. T. (1999), *Decolonizing Methodologies: Research and Indigenous Peoples*, London and New York & Dunedin, New Zealand: Zed Books & Otago University Press.

A landmark book on foregrounding Indigenous presence in research and on "researching back." The Introduction itself (1–18) is a powerful text which can be used in an undergraduate class.

Williams, C. (2016), "Maps have North at the Top, but It Could've Been Different," *BBC Future*, June 14, 2016, https://www.bbc.com/future/article/20160614-maps-have-north-at-the-top-but-it-couldve-been-different.

An accessible online article that introduces students to the history of north-up map orientation and discusses the contemporary social, political, and psychological significance of altering such orientation.

Wynter, S. (2003), "Unsettling the Coloniality of Being/Power/Truth/Freedom: Towards the Human, After Man, Its Overrepresentation—An Argument," *CR: The New Centennial Review*, 3 (3): 257–337.

Another important piece that shows how our ways of being human have to be explored outside the dominant understanding of the same, if one wishes to escape the coloniality of being imposed by the latter. Suitable for upper-level classes; excerpts can be used in an undergraduate class too.

Chapter 2

Conventional comparative philosophy has been largely confined to the classical traditions of China, India, and Japan. It has not sufficiently attended to how our understanding of "Chinese philosophy," "Indian philosophy," and "Japanese philosophy" has been influenced by the self-affirming practices of central Europe or to the specific contexts of the traditions studied, especially when these predate the industrial era. This chapter is a good place to begin making students aware of the specific context in which we philosophize. World philosophies could have been transmitted orally or through manuscripts; both modes are more amenable to changes in every step of the transmission process than in our predominant text culture.

Teaching Suggestions

- Have students review the course catalog and standard curriculum of their own department. How would an outside observer understand what philosophy is, based only on this department's course offerings? In what ways does the department reflect or resist the disciplinary eurocentrism we have discussed here?
- Invite students to draw up "their" philosophy family tree at the beginning and end of the term. Use these sketches to initiate a discussion about representation issues. Should philosophy as a discipline be diversified both in terms of content and practitioners?
- Encourage students to hold short presentations on philosophical topics in different languages. Does a different language help articulate philosophical issues that might be otherwise overlooked? Are there terms from European and Euro-American discourses that students find difficult to translate? Have students reflect on the limitations of allowing a single language to dominate philosophical discourse.
- Make students design one class which explicitly breaks away from ranking world cultures. Discuss the methods they have adopted to effectuate this departure.

Further Reading

Bernasconi, R. (2003), "Will the Real Kant Please Stand Up: The Challenge of Enlightenment Racism to the Study of the History of Philosophy," *Radical Philosophy*, (117): 13–22.

A much-cited spirited call to place canonical philosophers in their contexts, without "excising their racism." Can be used in an undergraduate class.

Kim, D. H. (2007), "What Is Asian American Philosophy?" in G. Yancy (ed.), *Philosophy in Multiple Voices*, 219–71, Lanham, etc.: Rowman & Littlefield.

Draws attention to the Orientalist underpinnings of classical Asian philosophy and argues for a modern Asian philosophy, which would include Asian American philosophy.

Eze, E. C. (1997), "The Color of Reason: The Idea of 'Race' in Kant's Anthropology," in E. C. Eze (ed.), *Postcolonial African Philosophy: A Critical Reader*, 103–40, Malden, Blackwell.

Analyses how Kant's transcendental philosophy is grounded in his views on race drawn from his thoughts on physical geography and anthropology.

Gordon, L. R. (2012), "Reasoning in Black: Africana Philosophy Under the Weight of Misguided Reason," *The Savannah Review*, (1): 81–96.

Argues that Africana philosophy, meaning philosophy of African-descent peoples, should be studied as a system of ideas. Easy to use in an undergraduate class.

Kalmanson, L. (2019), "Whiteness and the Construction of Buddhist Philosophy in Meiji Japan," in G. Yancy and E. McRae (eds.), *Buddhism and Whiteness: Critical Reflections*, 61–78, Lanham: Lexington.

A study of the racialized discourse that shaped the formation of "Buddhist philosophy" as a contemporary academic discipline.

Mattice, S. (2016), "Methodological Inspiration from Teaching Chinese Philosophy," in Sor-hoon Tan (ed.), *The Bloomsbury Research Handbook of Chinese Philosophy Methodologies*, 143–53, London, etc.: Bloomsbury.

Delivers useful suggestions in teaching Chinese philosophy such that students become aware of the different context(s) in which this tradition is practiced.

Mignolo, W. (2009), "Epistemic Disobedience, Independent Thought and Decolonial Freedom," *Theory, Culture & Society*, 26 (7–8): 159–81.

Influential text about shifting the geography of reason to unveil the geopolitics of knowledge-making practices.

Oggunaike, O. (2017), "African Philosophy Reconsidered: Africa, Religion, Race, and Philosophy," *Journal of Africana Religions*, 5 (2): 181–216.

An accessible academic essay that recounts the experiences of a young philosophy student of African descent navigating issues of eurocentrism in his engagement with work in African philosophy.

Shun, K.-L. (2016), "Methodological Reflections on the Study of Chinese Thought," in Sor-hoon Tan (ed.), *The Bloomsbury Research Handbook of Chinese Philosophy Methodologies*, 57–74, London, etc.: Bloomsbury.

Tries to show how philosophical construction can do justice to textual analysis and philosophical inquiry. Relatively easy to use in an undergraduate class if students are already familiar with methodological issues.

Sullivan, S. (2019), *White Privilege*, Cambridge, UK: Polity.

Easily accessible primer on white privilege and the concomitant nexus of race and class. Can be used as one preparatory reading for the course itself.

Van Norden, B. W. (2017), *Taking Back Philosophy: A Multicultural Manifesto*, New York: Columbia University Press.

Provides a series of arguments against eurocentrism in philosophy, which students can readily engage, in addition to offering many provocative claims about the role of philosophy in contemporary social and political life worldwide. This text can prompt students to explore the relevance of diversity in philosophy in contexts other than academia.

Chapter 3

Relational knowing promises to offer a fresh take on the study of world philosophies. To be able to explore its potential, students will first need to grasp how standard theory tends to operate with the notion of one unified, universal, and transcendental self. One might consider working with non-textual material, such as podcasts, or with historical material to effectuate this switch. Short and engaging texts provided by not-for-profit media outlets offer accessible material relating to alternate epistemological frameworks, the fallout of colonialism on education broadly construed, and philosophy in particular, and so on. Two useful websites for blogs and podcasts related to world philosophies include History of Philosophy without Any Gaps (https://historyofphilosophy.net) and The Deviant Philosopher (https://thedeviantphilosopher.org).

Teaching Suggestions

- Dividing the class into two groups, make the students discuss the view that group homogeneity is detrimental and not detrimental to the practice of professional philosophy.
- We have made the claim that academic philosophy today has been and continues to be dominated by the perspective of "white, male, propertied" scholars. Students will likely have encountered this claim in other contexts—for example, the "white male gaze" in film studies or literary theory. Invite students to become the "experts" in this discussion by bringing in the skills and resources they already possess as undergraduates to critically assess the state of academic philosophy. A larger project might invite them to participate in some data-driven research on topics such as demographics in academic publishing or the relative rankings of "mainstream" versus "specialized" (i.e., feminist, or cross-cultural) philosophy journals.
- Make the students map out conceptual-clusters of standard philosophical terms in small groups. Use these conceptual-clusters at the end of the course to initiate a discussion on terms from world philosophies that can be rendered and cannot be rendered meaningful with the help of these clusters.
- Design a class with the students in which a concentration technique is used to prepare students for reading a text, like the Ruist practices discussed in this chapter. Students might simply sit quietly before beginning their homework reading, or count their breaths, or listen to calming music. Discuss with students how they experienced the implementation of such a concentration technique.
- "We do not live inside our skins." Make groups find different formats in which they engage with this statement. Students might be encouraged to think about common English colloquialisms that speak to the permeability of personal and interpersonal experience,

such as "The room had a negative energy," or "I'm sending you good vibes," or "She has an unmistakable presence."

Further Reading

Geisz, S. (2016), "Body Practice and Meditation as Philosophy: Teaching Qigong, Taijiquan, and Yoga in College Courses," *Teaching Philosophy*, 39 (2): 115–35.

Directly addresses the role of Chinese contemplative and mind-body practices in the context of the undergraduate philosophical classroom.

Hall, D. L. (2001), "Just How Provincial Is Western Philosophy? 'Truth' in Comparative Context," *Social Epistemology: A Journal of Knowledge, Culture and Policy*, 15 (4): 285–97, DOI: 10.1080/02691720110093315.

Offers an intriguing take on the standard notion of truth being one provincial way to look at the world. Makes a case for approaching philosophical traditions through methods that are better suited to the tradition studied. Interestingly, he uses American pragmatism for this exercise.

Lugones, M. (2003), "Playfulness, 'World'-Traveling, and Loving Perception," in *Pilgrimages/Peregrinages: Theorizing Coalition Against Multiple Oppressions*, 77–100, Oxford etc.: Rowman and Littlefield.

A widely cited text about the need to travel to the different "worlds" constructed and inhabited by concrete, embodied people. Would complement the discussion of "knowing how" and "knowing that" well.

Mendoza, B. (2016), "Coloniality of Gender and Power: From Postcoloniality to Decoloniality," in L. Disch and M. Hawkesworth (eds.),

The Oxford Handbook of Feminist Theory, 100–21, New York, etc.: Oxford University Press.

Longish, informative article about anticolonial feminisms. Brings together postcolonial and decolonial work. Can be used in an undergraduate class for group work.

Mika, M. (2012), "'Overcoming Being' in Favour of Knowledge: The Fixing Effect of 'mātauranga,'" *Educational Philosophy and Theory*, 44 (10): 1080–92. DOI: 10.1111/j.1469-5812.2011.00771.x.

Makes a case for critical thinking in the application of eurocentric concepts to Māori ways of understanding the self's relation to the world.

Nagel, T. (1989), *The View from Nowhere*, Oxford: Oxford University Press.

This is a classic text that articulates the standard analytical conception of objectivity in epistemology, along with a look at some of the attendant problems and paradoxes. This book, or parts of it, can help students understand the mainstream meaning of the unified, universal, and transcendental self with whom we contrast the relational knower.

Sandoval, C. (2000), *Methodology of the Oppressed*, Minneapolis/London: University of Minnesota Press.

Works out a "methodology of the oppressed" which can allow for the development of new decolonial subjectivities.

Wang, R (2010), "The Virtuous Body at Work: The Ethical Life as *Qi* 氣 in Motion," *Dao*: *Journal of Comparative Philosophy*, 9 (3): 331–59.

Complements the discussion on *qi* (氣) in this chapter. Links up moral cultivation to bodily cultivation on a *qi*-based understanding of the body. Can be used in an upper-level class.

Chapter 4

Material referenced in this chapter can be used to shed light on how sociopolitical and epistemic dimensions intersect in a human endeavor like philosophy. Students may need more time to fruitfully engage with the claim that eurocentrism has worked as the epistemic structural principle of academic philosophy. Be open to the possibility that students may encounter this claim for the first time in their academic careers in your class. Work to create an atmosphere of trust to conduct this difficult, perhaps even uncomfortable, conversation. This can be an opportunity for teachers to develop and hone their own skills at relational knowing, inviting them to reflect not only on their own philosophical training but also on their sociopolitical location, gendered identity, class, race, and so forth.

Teaching Suggestions

- Have students use a standard website of an academic retailer to browse the tables of contents of various world religions textbooks, and to make notes about similarities and differences they find. Use this exercise to open a discussion about ways of mapping philosophical and religious traditions. This exercise might be paired with excerpts from Masuzawa's *Invention of World Religions* (2005), Park's *Africa, Asia, and the History of Philosophy* (2013), or, perhaps, a critical reading of Hegel's work (1995) in history of philosophy.
- Make students first find examples of "philosophical Euromonopolism" (Davis 2020) and then find formats through which they question, critique, and resist this monopolism.
- Co-organize a jam session with students about epistemic decolonization in and out of campus. Make them compare both these experiences.

Further Reading

Arisaka, Y. (1997), "Beyond 'East' and 'West': Nishida's Universalism and Postcolonial Critique," *Review of Politics*, 59 (3): 541–60.

Examines how Japanese philosophy's self-positioning against eurocentrism led to one formulation of an explicit anti-eurocentrism, which though "became entangled" in the imperialist regime. Can be used in an upper-level class.

Dirlik, A. (2000), "Confounding Metaphors, Inventions of the World: What Is World History For?," *The Review of Education/Pedagogy/Cultural Studies*, 22 (4): 323–67. DOI:10.1080/1071441000220403.

A critical piece of historical scholarship, which argues that the term "eurocentrism" should be made more specific. Calls out the "global internalization" of eurocentrism.

Karatani, K. (1991), "The Discursive Space of Modern Japan," *boundary*, 2 (18): 191–219.

Another critical piece of scholarship that brings to the fore the arbitrariness of periodization. Argues that nations construct communal worlds/eras through historical narrations. These worlds exist simultaneously and are interrelated.

Outlaw, Jr., L. (1997), "Africana Philosophy," *Journal of Ethics*, 1 (3): 265–90.

Author has been influential in shaping Africana philosophy as a "gathering notion." An important, contemporary document in understanding the making of this concept.

Park, J. Y. (2017), *Women and Buddhist Philosophy: Engaging Zen Master Kim Iryŏp*, Honolulu: University of Hawai'i Press.

This book can be useful to both teachers and students in thinking about their own personal location in relation to philosophical study. Throughout the book, Park explores autobiographical writing and personal memoir as forms of philosophical production.

Presby, G. (2002), "Maasai Concepts of Personhood: The Roles of Recognition, Community, and Individuality," *International Studies in Philosophy*, 34 (2): 57–82.

A fascinating and nuanced account of Maasai personhood, which critiques the view that Euro-American societies are individualistic and African communitarian. Argues that this binary confuses ontology with evaluation. Easy to use in an undergraduate class.

Salles, A. and Millán-Zaibert, E. ed. (2005), *The Role of History in Latin American Philosophy: Contemporary Perspectives*, New York: State University of New York.

Brings together several contemporary scholars who shed light on historical reasons that lead to a devaluation of Latin American philosophy, arguing that the devaluation of this tradition in the academy is not warranted.

Wiredu, K. (2002), "Conceptual Decolonization as an Imperative in Contemporary African Philosophy: Some Personal Reflections," *Collège International de Philosophie*, 2 (36): 53–64.

An important text that appeals to African philosophers to be more attentive to their *African* identity when they philosophize about Africa. Grounds this call for a conceptual decolonization by observing how many of us are "up to our necks" in Euro-American "metaphysical and religious assumptions." Easy to use in an undergraduate class.

Chapter 5

After students have understood that the standard narration of philosophy is not as plausible as made out to be (see Chapter 2), it should be easier for them to grasp that the standard narrations about other world philosophies may not be wholly coherent either. It may be useful to use the referenced material to highlight how our understanding of individual disciplines is interdisciplinary. Geography props up history, which in turn props up philosophy.

Teaching Suggestions

- Use a globe to visualize how philosophical traditions have been labelled in the past. Initiate a class discussion on why certain traditions are linked up with the names of modern nation-states, others with continents, others with ethnicities, and yet others with religions.
- As a way to scale down the "dream department" assignment discussed in this chapter, ask students to develop a "dream syllabus" for an introductory course reflecting a curriculum in world philosophies.
- Invite students to develop a class session using this relational knower. Typical student-led class sessions often involve either a solo presentation, a group presentation, or a student-run discussion that tends to find "discussion leaders" standing at the front of the room posing a series of questions to the class. Have students reflect on their own go-to strategies for completing such student-led classroom assignments. What changes might they make to enact more relational ways of knowing?

Further Reading

Asad, T. (1986), *The Idea of an Anthropology of Islam*, Occasional Papers, Washington, DC: Center for Contemporary Arab Studies, Georgetown University.

Important account of Islam as a discursive tradition written by an anthropologist. Asad argues that every representation of a living tradition is contestable, and should be seen as such. The essay with the same title as the book is short and lucid. See 1–22.

Barlas, A. (2019), *Believing Women in Islam: Unreading Patriarchal Interpretations of the Qu'ran*, Revised Edition, Austin: University of Texas Press.

A nuanced reading in unreading patriarchy. Chapter 6 can be used in an undergraduate class to illustrate the Qu'ran's endorsement of a genderless God while acknowledging the specificity of female bodies.

El-Rouayheb, K. and Schmidtke, S. (2017), *The Oxford Handbook of Islamic Philosophy*, Oxford: Oxford University Press.

Organized in chronological order. Each paper focuses on one specific text by a famous philosopher. Can be consulted with the Routledge Companion.

Ganeri, J. ed. (362017), *Oxford Handbook of Indian Philosophy*, New York, etc.: Oxford University Press.

A first attempt at integrating sources from the non-Sanskritic Indian subcontinent under the umbrella of Indian philosophy. Includes articles that stress a heightened methodological awareness of the manner in which our concepts frame our inquiry.

Kaukua, J. (2015), *Self-Awareness in Islamic Philosophy: Avicenna and Beyond*, Cambridge: Cambridge University Press.

Tracks the developments in the study of self-awareness that are remarkable in philosophy in the Islamic context.

Mignolo, W. (2003), "Philosophy and the Colonial Difference," in Eduardo Mendieta (ed.), *Latin American Philosophy: Currents, Issues, Debates*, 80–9, Bloomington: Indiana University Press.

An important text by Mignolo, which questions whether the notion of "culture" itself, as a category, is a colonial construction. This essay would be helpful in prompting students to dig down to the generic categories they may take for granted as self-evident, but which in fact have an intellectual history marked by shifting power dynamics (as do categories such as "race" and "gender" as well as "philosophy" itself).

Narayan, U. (1998), "Essence of Culture and a Sense of History: A Feminist Critique of Cultural Essentialism," *Hypatia*, 13 (2): 86–106.

An influential text that argues against the widespread view that cultures are like discrete, easily distinguishable "packages." Warns that the "pseudoparticularism" involved in such claims may reflect hegemonic views of what is particular to a specific culture.

Raghuramaraju, A. (2012), "Introduction," in A. Raghuramaraju, *Enduring Colonialism: Classical Presences and Modern Absences in Indian Philosophy*, 1–26, New Delhi, etc.: Oxford University Press.

Identifies the contemporary lack of texts and systems of philosophy in India as emanating from a sensitivity to contemporality. Can be used to draw attention to the standard, erroneous construction of Indian philosophy according to which this tradition is merely of historical worth.

Taylor, R. C. and López-Farjeat, L. X., ed. (2016), *The Routledge Companion to Islamic Philosophy*, London and New York: Routledge.

Handy companion organized by philosophical fields and issues. Can be consulted with the *Oxford Handbook* mentioned earlier.

Notes

Chapter 2

1 https://tibet.emory.edu/about/index.html
2 https://voices.uchicago.edu/buddhiststudies/
3 https://philosophy.unm.edu/index.html
4 https://hawaii.edu/phil/
5 Josephson-Storm previously published works under the name Josephson alone. Although we refer to him by his current name in the text, in our list of references his 2012 and 2006 works are alphabetized by the name under which he published them.
6 In this passage, Kongzi famously declares himself a follower of the ways of the Zhou dynasty (1046–256 BCE).
7 Notably, Inoue thought that ultimately only Buddhism provided the most direct path to the full, lived experience of the absolute (Josephson 2006: 159).

Chapter 3

1 See Krishnamurthy et al. (2017), Schwitzgebel and Dicey Jennings (2017), also Olberding (2017). For some first-person accounts, see Shorter Bourhanou (2017) and Piper (2019).
2 Notably, postcolonial knowledge making is for Verran a two-way affair. In the example narrated earlier, both the scientist and the landowner should make room for this epistemic disconcertment.
3 Both Ruism (*rujia* 儒家) and Daoism (*daojia* 道家) are associated with some of China's earliest texts, the so-called Five Classics in the case of Ruism, and the *Daodejing* (道德經) and *Zhuangzi* (莊子) in the case of

Daoism. The earliest of the Five Classics, the *Yijing* (易經), dates back to the Western Zhou period (1000–750 BCE) and the *Daodejing* to at least the Warring States (402–221 BCE). The *Yijing* and the *Daodejing* share what we might call a *qi*-based cosmology, or a theory according to which an initial state of formless matter-energy (*qi* 氣) gives rise to the complex world we now inhabit through a series of differentiations, beginning with the initial distinction into *yin* (隱) and *yang* (陽).

4 A version of the material that follows also appears in Kalmanson (2020), which addresses additional philosophical—specifically existential—implications of this conception of the mind.

5 For an English version, see Ian Johnston and Wang Ping (trans.) (2012: 139).

6 Our translation largely follows, with modification, Garder (trans.) (1990: 145).

7 See Garder (trans.) (1990: 145).

8 See Gardner (trans.) (1990: 137–8).

Chapter 4

1 In Bashir's view, Hodgson's posthumously published volumes on *The Venture in Islam* (1974) continue to perceive Islam as a "timeless entity that exists apart from the thoughts, actions, and circumstances of Muslims who profess belief in it" (Bashir 2014: 527).

2 This is similar to the rhetorical force of Jay L. Garfield's and Bryan W. Van Norden's claim that what we now call simply "philosophy" should be called "European and American philosophy," if the discipline will not otherwise diversify itself (Garfield and Van Norden 2016).

3 We do not mean to diminish the important work that Huston Smith has contributed to religious literacy and interfaith dialogue. We also note that a deeper search of textbooks or introductions to world religions will turn up some volumes that resist, in one way or another,

the pattern that we discuss regarding the chapters on "primal," "native," or similarly designated traditions. However, our general claim still stands: many common and well-reviewed textbooks present students with the basic pattern that Masuzawa critiques.

4 Masuzawa focuses on debates about the nature of Buddhism by European scholars to illustrate the contentious discourses surrounding the question of which traditions belonged in the ranks of "world religions" (2005, especially the fourth chapter).

Chapter 5

1 See Kirloskar-Steinbach (2018).

2 Iqbal refers to Prophet Muhammad's prophecy that Islam would fall into several sects, out of which only one would be right. As Diagne points out, there is another variation about seventy-three sects too, which Al-Ghazālī (ca. 1056–1111) uses (2010: 32).

3 In the Indian language Marathi, the term "dalit" literally means "downtrodden." Bhimrao Ambedkar (1891–1956), the famous drafter of the Indian constitution, translated it as "broken men." Today, it is used as a term of self-identification by members of the erstwhile lower castes, who were—and continue to be—subjected to caste domination.

4 See Jenco (2007) and Kalmanson (2017).

Conclusion

1 For more discussion of Kim's article and the issues at stake, see Kalmanson (2015).

References

Adler, J. (2004), "Varieties of Spiritual Experience: *Shen* in Neo-Confucian Discourse," in T. Wei-ming and M. E. Tucker (eds.), *Confucian Spirituality*, Vol. 2, 120–48, New York: Crossroad.

Ames, R. T. (2011), *Confucian Role Ethics: A Vocabulary*, Honolulu: University of Hawai'i Press.

Anderson, K., Ruiz, E. F., Stewart, G., and Tlostanova, M. (2019), "What Can Indigenous Feminist Knowledge and Practices Bring to "Indigenizing the Academy?" *Journal of World Philosophies*, 4 (1): 121–55.

Baba, E. (2017), "*Zhijue* as Appreciation and Realization in Zhu Xi: An Examination through Hun and Po," *Philosophy East and West*, 67 (2): 301–17.

Barker, P. (2017), "The Social Structure of Islamicate Science," *Journal of World Philosophies*, (2): 37–47.

Bashir, S. (2014), "On Islamic Time: Rethinking Chronology in the Historiography of Islamic Societies," *History and Theory*, 53 (4): 519–44.

Bashir, S. (2017), "Eurocentrism, Islam and the Intellectual Politics of Civilizational Framing," *InterDisciplines: Journal of History and Sociology*, 8 (2): 21–36.

Berger, D. L. (2015), *Encounters of Mind: Luminosity and Personhood in Indian and Chinese Thought*, Albany: SUNY Press.

Bernasconi, R. (1998), "Stuck Inside of Mobile with the Memphis Blues Again: Interculturalism and the Conversation of Races," in C. Willett (ed.), *Theorizing Multiculturalism: A Guide to the Current Debate*, 276–98, Malden, MA: Blackwell.

Bernasconi, R. (2003), "Will the Real Kant Please Stand Up: The Challenge of Enlightenment Racism to the Study of the History of Philosophy," *Radical Philosophy*, 117: 13–22.

Bhattacharya, K. (1984 [1931]), "Svaraj in Ideas," *Indian Philosophical Quarterly*, 11 (4): 383–93.

Bourhanou, J. S. (2017), "Legitimizing Blacks in Philosophy," *Journal of World Philosophies*, 2 (2): 27–36.

Bowker, J. (2006), *World Religions*, London: DK Press.

Brooks, T. (2013), "Philosophy Unbound: The Idea of Global Philosophy," *Metaphilosophy*, 44 (3): 254–66.

Bruya, B. (2017), "Ethnocentrism and Multiculturalism in Contemporary Philosophy," *Philosophy East and West*, 67 (4): 991–1018.

Campany, R. F. (2003), "On the Very Idea of Religions (in the Modern West and in Early Medieval China)," *History of Religions*, 42 (4): 287–319.

Connolly, T. (2015), *Doing Philosophy Comparatively*, New York and London: Bloomsbury.

Cooper, D. (2018), "From World Philosophies to Existentialism—And Back," *Journal of World Philosophies*, (3): 105–9. doi: 10.2979/jourworlphil.3.2.08.

Creller, A. (2018), *Making Space for Knowing: A Capacious Approach to Comparative Epistemology*, Lanham, MD: Lexington Books.

Cusicanqui, S. R. (2012), "Ch'ixinakax utxiwa: A Reflection on the Practices and Discourses of Decolonization," *The South Atlantic Quarterly*, 111 (1): 95–109.

Dalai Lama [Tenzin Gyatso], Khonton Peljor Lhundrub, and Jose Ignacio Cabezon (2011), *Meditation on the Nature of Mind*, Somerville, MA: Wisdom Publications, 2011.

Dalmiya, V. and Martín Alcoff, L. (1993), "Are 'Old Wives' Tales' Justified?" in L. Martín Alcoff and E. Potter (eds.), *Feminist Epistemologies*, 217–44, New York: Routledge.

Dalmiya, V. (2016), *Caring to Know: Comparative Care Ethics, Feminist Epistemology, and the Mahābhārata*, New Delhi: Oxford University Press.

Davis, B. W. (2020), "Introduction: What Is Japanese Philosophy?" in B. W. Davis (ed.), *The Oxford Handbook of Japanese Philosophy*, 1–79, New York: Oxford.

Daya Krishna (1986), "Comparative Philosophy: What It Is and What It Ought to Be," *Diogenes*, (34): 58–69.

Diagne, S. B. (2010), *Islam and Open Society: Fidelity and Movement in the Philosophy of Muhammad Iqbal*, trans. Melissa McMahon, Dakar: CODESRIA.

Diagne, S. B. (2018), *Open to Reason: Muslim Philosophers in Conversation with the Western Tradition*, New York: Columbia University Press.

Donahue, A. (2016), "For the Cowherds: Coloniality and Conventional Truth in Buddhist Philosophy," *Philosophy East and West*, 66 (2): 597–617.

Druart, T.-A. (2004), "Philosophy in Islam," in A. S. McGrade (ed.), *The Cambridge Companion to Medieval Philosophy*, 97–120, Cambridge, etc.: Cambridge University Press.

Du Toit, L. and Coetzee, A. (2017), "Gendering African Philosophy; Or: African Feminism as Decolonising Force," in A. Afolayan and T. Falola (eds.), *Palgrave Handbook of African Philosophy*, 333–47, New York: Palgrave Macmillan.

El-Bizri, N. (2010), "The Labyrinth of Philosophy in Islam," *Comparative Philosophy*, 1 (2): 3–23.

El-Bizri, N. (2016), "Falsafa. A Labyrinth of Theory and Method," *Synthesis Philosophica*, 62 (2): 295–311.

Eze, E. C. (1997), "The Color of Reason: The Idea of 'Race' in Kant's Anthropology," in E. C. Eze (ed.), *Postcolonial African Philosophy: A Critical Reader*, 103–40, Malden: Blackwell.

Eze, E. C. (2001), "African Philosophy and the Analytic Tradition," *Philosophical Papers*, 30 (3): 205–13.

Ganeri, J. (2016), "A Manifesto for Re:emergent Philosophy," Confluence: Online *Journal of World Philosophies* (4): 134–42. URL: https://scholarworks.iu.edu/iupjournals/index.php/confluence/article/view/561/66.

Ganeri, J. (2017), "Why Indian Philosophy? Why Now?," in J. Ganeri (ed.), *The Oxford Handbook of Indian Philosophy*, 1–12, New York: Oxford.

Ganeri, J. (2019), "Epistemic Pluralism: From Systems to Stances," *Journal of the American Philosophical Association*, 5 (1): 1–21.

Gardner, D. K., trans. (1990), *Learning to Be a Sage: Selection from the Conversations of Master Chu, Arranged Topically*, Berkeley: University of California Press.

Garfield, J. L. and Van Norden, B. W. (2016), "If Philosophy Won't Diversify, Let's Call It What It Really Is," May 11. Available online: https://www.nytimes.com/2016/05/11/opinion/if-philosophy-wont-diversify-lets-call-it-what-it-really-is.html (accessed January 12, 2020).

Guru, G. and Sarukkai, S. (2012), *The Cracked Mirror: An Indian Debate on Experience and Theory*, Delhi: Oxford University Press.

Gurukkal, R. (2013), "On Mirroring the Social: Can Felt-Ontology Alone Inform the Theory?" *Economic and Political Weekly*, 48 (14): 27–31.

Gutas, D. (2002), "The Study of Arabic Philosophy in the Twentieth Century: An Essay on the Historiography of Arabic Philosophy," *British Journal of Middle Eastern Studies*, 29 (1): 5–25.

Gyekye, K. (2010), "Person and Community in Akan Thought," in K. Wiredu and K. Gyekye (eds.), *Person and Community: Ghanaian Perspectives I*, 101–22, Washington: Council for Research in Values and Philosophy.

Hegel, G. W. F. (1995), *Lectures on the History of Philosophy: Greek Philosophy to Plato*, trans. E. S. Haldane, Lincoln: University of Nebraska Press.

Hodgson, M. G. S. (1993), *Rethinking World History: Essays on Europe, Islam and World History*, Cambridge: Cambridge University Press.

Hughes, A. (2013), *Muslim Identities: An Introduction to Islam*, New York: Columbia University Press.

Ikuenobe, P. (2017), "Matolino's Misunderstanding of Menkiti's African Moral View of the Person and Community," *South African Journal of Philosophy*, 36 (4): 553–67.

Iqbal, M. (1920), *The Secrets of the Self (Asrār-I Khudī): A Philosophical Poem, Translated from the Original Persian, with Introduction and Notes*, London, etc.: Macmillan and Co.

Iqbal, M. (1954 [1934]), *The Reconstruction of Religious Thought in Islam*, Lahore: Shaikh Muhammad Ashraf.

Janz, Bruce B. (1996), "Alterity, Dialogue, and African Philosophy," in E. C. Eze (ed.), *Postcolonial African Philosophy: A Critical Reader*, Oxford: Blackwell Publishers.

Jenco, L. (2011), "Recentering Political Theory: The Promise of Mobile Locality," *Cultural Critique*, 79 (Fall): 27–59.

Jenco, L. (2016), "Methods from Within the Chinese Tradition," in S. Tan (ed.), *The Bloomsbury Research Handbook of Chinese Philosophy Methodologies*, 273–88, London: Bloomsbury.

Jenco, L. K. (2007), ,"'What Does Heaven Ever Say?' A Methods-Centered Approach to Cross-Cultural Engagement," *The American Political Science Review*, 101 (4): 741–55.

Johnston, I. and Wang, P., trans. (2012), *Daxue and Zhongyong: Bilingual Edition*, Hong Kong: The Chinese University Press.

Josephson, J. Ā. (2006), "When Buddhism Became a 'Religion': Religion and Superstition in the Writings of Inoue Enryō," *Japanese Journal of Religious Studies*, 33 (1): 143–68.

Josephson, J. Ā. (2012), *The Invention of Religion in Japan*, Chicago: University of Chicago Press.

Josephson-Storm, J. Ā. (2018), "The Superstition, Secularism, and Religion Trinary: Or Re-Theorizing Secularism," *Method and Theory in the Study of Religion*, 30 (1): 1–20.

Kalmanson, L. (2015), "If You Show Me Yours: Reading All 'Difference' as 'Colonial Difference' in Comparative Philosophy," *Comparative Philosophy and Continental Philosophy*, 7 (2): 201–13.

Kalmanson, L. (2017), "The Ritual Methods of Comparative Philosophy," *Philosophy East and West*, 67 (2): 399–418.

Kalmanson, L. (2020), *Cross-Cultural Existentialism: On the Meaning of Life in Asian and Western Thought*, London: Bloomsbury.

Kim, D. (2007), "What Is Asian American Philosophy?" in George Yancy (ed.), *Philosophy in Multiple Voices*, 219–72, Lanham: Rowman and Littlefield.

Kim, D. (2019), "Alterity, Analectics, and the Challenges of Epistemic Decolonization," *The Southern Journal of Philosophy, Spindel Supplement*, (57): 37–62.

Kim, Y. S. (2015), "Zhu Xi on Scientific and Occult Subjects: Defining and Extending the Boundaries of Confucian Learning," in David Jones and Jinli He (eds.), *Returning to Zhu Xi: Emerging Patterns Within the Supreme Polarity*, 121–46, Albany: SUNY Press.

King, R. (2009), "Philosophy of Religion as Border Control: Globalization and the Decolonization of the 'Love of Wisdom' (Philosophia)," in P. Bilimoria and A. B. Irvine (eds.), *Postcolonial Philosophy of Religion*, 35–53, Dordrecht: Springer etc.

Kirloskar-Steinbach, M. (2018), "Representing Indian Philosophy Through the Nation: An Exploration of the Public Philosopher Radhakrishnan," *Sophia: International Journal of Philosophy and Traditions*, 57 (3): 375–87.

Kirloskar-Steinbach, M., Ramana, G., and Maffie, J. (2014), "Introducing Confluence: A Thematic Essay," *Confluence*, 1: 7–63.

Krishnamurthy, M., Liao, S.-Y., Deveaux, M., and Dalecki, M. (2017), "The Underrepresentation of Women in Prestigious Ethics Journals," *Hypatia*, 32 (4): 928–39.

Larson, G. J. (1987), "'Conceptual Resources' in South Asia for 'Environmental Ethics' or the Fly Is Still Alive and Well in the Bottle," *Philosophy East and West*, (37): 150–7.

Lebakeng, J. T. et al. (2006), "Epistemicide, Institutional Cultures and Imperative for the Africanisation of Universities in South Africa," *Alternation*, 13 (1): 70–87.

Lugones, M. (2010), "Toward a Decolonial Feminism," *Hypatia*, 25 (4): 742–59.

Lugones, M. and Spelman, E. (1983), "Have We Got a Theory for You! Feminist Theory, Cultural Imperialism, and the Demand for the 'Woman's Voice,'" *Women's Studies International Forum*, 6 (6): 573–81.

Lunyu 論語 (2011), in D. Sturgeon (ed.), *Chinese Text Project*, https://ctext.org/analects/zh.

Madaio, J. (2017), "Re-thinking Neo-Vedānta: Swami Vivekananda and the Selective Historiography of Advaita Vedānta," *Religions*, 8 (101): 1–12.

Maraldo, J. C. (2011), "Beginnings, Definitions, Disputations: Overview," in J. W. Heisig, T. P. Kasulis, and J. C. Maraldo (eds.), *Japanese Philosophy: A Sourcebook*, 553–69, Honolulu: University of Hawai'i Press.

Maraldo, J. C.ジョン・マラルド (2014), "Nihon no kindai shoki ni okeru seiyō tetsugaku no sesshu" 日本の近代初期における西洋哲学の摂取 [The reception of Western philosophy in early modern Japan], trans. (from the English) Shirai Masato白井雅人, *International Inoue Enryo Research*, (2): 200–16.

Martín Alcoff, L. (1995), "The Problem of Speaking for Others," in J. Roof and R. Wiegman (eds.), *Who Can Speak? Authority and Critical Identity*, 97–119, Chicago: University of Illinois Press.

Martín Alcoff, L. (2017), "Philosophy and Philosophical Practice: Eurocentrism as an Epistemology of Ignorance," in I. J. Kidd, J. Medina, and G. Pohlhaus, Jr. (eds.), *The Routledge Handbook of Epistemic Injustice*, 397–408, London and New York: Routledge.

Masson-Oursel, P. (1951), "True Philosophy Is Comparative Philosophy," Harold E. McCarthy, trans., *Philosophy East and West*, 1 (1): 6–9.

Masuzawa, T. (2005), *The Invention World Religions: Or How European Universalism Was Preserved in the Language of Pluralism*, Chicago: Chicago University Press.

Matolino, B. (2011), "The (Mal) Function of "It" in Ifeanyi Menkiti's Normative Account of Person," *African Studies Quarterly*,12 (4): 23–37.

Matolino, B. (2018), "The Shaping of the Future of African Philosophy," in E. E. Etieyibo (ed.), *Method, Substance, and the Future of African Philosophy*, 335–53, Cham: Palgrave Macmillan.

Mattice, S. A. (2014), *Metaphor and Metaphilosophy: Philosophy as Combat, Play, and Aesthetic Experience*, Lanham, etc: Lexington Books.

Mayar, M. and Guevara González, Y. (2017), "Introduction: Done with Eurocentrism? Unpacking a Plural Construct," *InterDisciplines: Journal of History and Sociology*, 8 (2): 1–20.

Meighoo, S. (2016), *The End of the West and Other Cautionary Tales*, New York: Columbia University Press.

Menkiti, I. A. (1984), "Person and Community in African Traditional Thought," in R. Wright (ed.), *African Philosophy, an Introduction*, 171–81, Lanham, MD: University Press of America.

Menkiti, I. A. (2005), "On the Normative Conception of a Person," in K. Wiredu (ed.), *A Companion to African Philosophy*, 324–31, Malden: Blackwell Publishers.

Mika, C. (2017), *Indigenous Education and the Metaphysics of Presence*, London and New York: Routledge.

Miller, J. (2017), *China's Green Religion: Daoism and the Quest for a Sustainable Future*, New York: Columbia University Press.

Mills, C. W. (2017), *Black Rights, White Wrongs: The Critique of Racial Liberalism*, Oxford, etc: Oxford University Press.

Mills, C. W. (1988), "Alternative Epistemologies," *Social Theory and Practice*, 14: 237–63.

Mills, C. W. (2007), "White Ignorance," in S. Sullivan, and N. Tuana (eds.), *Race and Epistemologies of Ignorance*, 13–38, Albany: State University of New York Press.

Mohanty, J. (1982), "Indian Philosophy Between Tradition and Modernity," in S. S. Rama Rao Pappu and R. Puligandla (eds.), *Indian Philosophy: Past and Future*, 233–52, Delhi, etc: Motilal Banarsidass.

Monahan, M. J. (2011), *The Creolizing Subject: Race, Reason, and the Politics of Purity*, New York: Fordham University Press.

Morisato, T. (2019), *Faith and Reason in Continental and Japanese Philosophy: Reading Tanabe Hajime and William Desmond*, London etc.: Bloomsbury.

Mungwini, P. (2013), "African Modernities and the Critical Reappropriation of Indigenous Knowledges: Towards a Polycentric Global Epistemology," *International Journal of African Renaissance Studies - Multi-, Inter- and Transdisciplinarity*, 8 (1): 78–93.

Mungwini, P. (2017), "'African Know Thyself': Epistemic Injustice and the Quest for Liberative Knowledge," *International Journal of African Renaissance Studies - Multi-, Inter-and Transdisciplinarity*, 12 (2): 5–18.

Nicholson, A. J. (2011), *Unifying Hinduism: Philosophy and Identity in Indian Intellectual History*, New Delhi: Permanent Black.

Nylan, M. (2016), "Academic Silos, or 'What I Wish Philosophers Knew About Early China," in Sor-hoon Tan (ed.), *The Bloomsbury Research Handbook of Chinese Philosophy Methodologies*, 91–114, London, etc: Bloomsbury.

Olberding, A. (2017), "Philosophical Exclusion and Conversational Practices," *Philosophy East and West*, 67 (4): 1023–38.

Oritsegbubemi, O. A. and Yurkivska, O. (2014), "Can a Communitarian Concept of African Personhood be Both Relational and Gender-Neutral?" *South African Journal of Philosophy*, 33 (1): 85–99.

Ortega, M. (2016), *In-between: Latina Feminist Phenomenology, Multiplicity and the Self*, Albany: SUNY.

Outlaw, Jr., L. (1996), *On Race and Philosophy*, New York and London: Routledge.

Outlaw, Jr., L. (1998), "'Multiculturalism,' Citizenship, Education, and American Liberal Democracy," in C. Willett (ed.), *Theorizing Multiculturalism: A Guide to the Current Debate*, 382–97, Malden, MA: Blackwell.

Oyěwùmí, O. (1999), "Multiculturalism or Multibodism: On the Impossible Intersections of Race and Gender in American White Feminist and Black Nationalist Discourse," *Western Journal of Black Studies*, 23 (3): 182–9.

Oyěwùmí, O. (2011), "Decolonizing the Intellectual and the Quotidian: Yorùbá Scholars(hip) and Male Dominance," in O. Oyěwùmí (ed.),

Gender Epistemologies in Africa: Gendering Traditions, Spaces, Social Institutions, and Identities, 9–33, New York: Palgrave Macmillan.

Park, P. K. J. (2013), *Africa, Asia, and the History of Philosophy*, Albany: State University of New York Press.

Partridge, C. (2018), *Introduction to World Religions*, 3rd ed., Minneapolis: Fortress Press.

Piper, A. (2019), "Philosophy En Route to Reality: A Bumpy Ride," *Journal of World Philosophies*, 4 (2): 106–18.

Radhakrishnan, S. (1951), "On Philosophical Synthesis," *Philosophy East and West*, (1): 4.

Raghuramaraju, A. (2010), "Problematising Lived Dalit Experience," *Economic and Political Weekly*, 45 (29): 162–67.

Ram-Prasad, C. (2018), *Human Being, Bodily Being: Phenomenology from Classical India*, Oxford, UK: Oxford University Press.

Rivera, O. (2019), *Delimitations of Latin American Philosophy: Beyond Redemption*, Bloomington: Indiana University Press.

Rosemont, Jr., H. (1988), "Against Relativism," in G. J. Larson and E. Deutsch (eds.), *Interpreting Across Boundaries: New Essays in Comparative Philosophy*, 36–63, Princeton, NJ, etc.: Princeton University Press.

Rosemont, Jr., H. (2004), "Which Rights? Whose Democracy? A Confucian Critique of the Western Liberal Tradition," in K. Shun, and D. Wong (eds.), *Confucian Ethics: A Comparative Study of Self, Autonomy, and Community*, 49–71, Cambridge, etc.: Cambridge University Press.

Rosemont, Jr., H. and R. T. Ames (2016), *Confucian Role Ethics: A Moral Vision for the 21st Century?* Taipei: National Taiwan University Press.

Rosenlee, L. L. (2006), *Confucianism and Women: A Philosophical Interpretation*, Albany: State University of New York Press.

Salkever, S. and Nylan, M. (1994), "Comparative Political Philosophy and Liberal Education: 'Looking for Friends in History,'" *Political Science and Politics*, 27 (2): 238–47.

Satyanarayana, K. (2013), "Experience and Dalit Theory," *Comparative Studies of South Asia, Africa and the Middle East*, 33 (3): 398–402.

Schutte, O. (2000), "Continental Philosophy and Postcolonial Subjects," *Philosophy Today*, (44): 8–17 (Supplement: Philosophy in Body, Culture, and Time).

Schwitzgebel, E. and Dicey Jennings, C. (2017), "Women in Philosophy: Quantitative Analyses of Specialization, Prevalence, Visibility, and Generational Change," *Public Affairs Quarterly*, 31: 83–105.

Scott, D. (2012), "The Traditions of Historical Others," *Symposia on Gender, Race and Philosophy*, 8 (1): 1–8.

Serequeberhan, T. (1994), *The Hermeneutics of African Philosophy: Horizon and Discourse*, New York: Routledge.

Sjödin, A.-P. (2011), "Conceptualizing Philosophical Tradition: A Reading of Wilhelm Halbfass, Daya Krishna, and Jitendranath Mohanty," *Philosophy East and West*, 61 (3): 534–46.

Smart, N. (1999), *World Philosophies*, London: Routledge.

Smith, H. (2009), *The World's Religions*, New York: HarperOne.

Smith, L. T. (1999), *Decolonizing Methodologies: Research and Indigenous Peoples*, London: Zed Books.

Solomon, R. C. and Higgins, K. M. (2003), "Introduction," in R. C. Solomon, and K. M. Higgins (eds.), *From Africa to Zen: An Invitation to World Philosophy*, ix–xvi, Lanham, etc.: Rowman and Littlefield Publishers.

Starblanket, G. and Kiiwetinepinesiik Stark, H. (2018), "Toward a Relational Paradigm—Four Points for Consideration: Knowledge, Gender, Land and Modernity," in M Asch, J. Borrows and J. Tully (eds.), *Resurgence and Reconciliation: Indigenous-Settler Relations and Earth Teachings*, 175–207, Toronto: University of Toronto Press.

Stewart, G. (2017), "The 'Hau' of Research: Mauss Meets Kaupapa Māori," *Journal of World Philosophies*, 2 (1): 1–11.

Stewart, G. (2010), *Good Science? The Growing Gap between Power and Education*, Rotterdam, etc.: Sense Publishers.

Tully, J. (2014), *On Global Citizenship: James Tully in Dialogue*, London and New York: Bloomsbury Academic.

Van Norden, B. W. (2017), *Taking Back Philosophy: A Multicultural Manifesto*, New York: Columbia University Press.

Verran, H. (2013), "Engagement between Disparate Knowledge Traditions: Toward Doing Difference Generatively and in Good Faith," in L. Green (ed.), *Contested Ecologies: Dialogues in the South on Nature and Knowledge*, 141–61, Cape Town: HRSC Press.

Waters, A. (2001), "Language Matters-A Metaphysic of NonDiscreet NonBinary Dualism," *American Philosophical Association Newsletter on American Indians in Philosophy*, 1 (2): 5–14.

Wiredu, K. (1998), "Can Philosophy Be Intercultural? An African Viewpoint," *Diogenes*, 46 (184): 147–67.

Yampolsky, Philip B., trans. (2012), *The Platform Sutra of the Sixth Patriarch*, New York: Columbia University Press.

Zhu X. 朱熹 (2011a), *Daxue Zhang Ju* 大學章句, in Donald Sturgeon (ed.), Chinese Text Project, https://ctext.org/si-shu-zhang-ju-ji-zhu/da-xue-zhang-ju.

Zhu X. 朱熹 (2011b), *Zhuzi yulei* 朱子語類, in Donald Sturgeon (ed.), Chinese Text Project, http://ctext.org/zhuzi-yulei/zh.

Index